THE
NEXT
MESSI

FROM BACKYARDS TO BIG LEAGUES

MAX GOALMAN

First edition, 2024.
www.maxgoalman.com

CONTENTS

CHAPTER 1
Ghouls and Goals

"Starting something new is like a one-person game of Jenga — just when you think you've got it all together, everything falls apart again!"

— MR. BEAST

Books are boring. So why am I writing one?

Technically, I'm writing a journal. That's what Dad calls it. He says writing in this journal will help me put things into perspective. How come adults are always going on and on about perspective, anyway? I'm not even sure what it means exactly.

At any rate, here I am. Putting my pen to paper and spilling my guts out onto the screen. What should I write first?

My name is Max. I'm twelve years old and live on the quietest street in the sleepiest town you've ever seen. Literally, nothing ever happens here. We have to make our own fun.

I really want to talk about the huge, mega-giant thing

that happened to me today...but Dad says I can't do that right at the start. He says I have to 'set the stage' first. So here it goes.

This morning my alarm blared me awake. I fumbled around on the nightstand without opening my eyes until I hit the off switch. You know what I hate about mornings? They come so darn early.

I looked at the sunlight coming in through my bedroom window. Something didn't feel right.

Wait, it's Saturday, I thought. *Why did I bother to set an alarm on a Saturday?*

My brain was still half snoozing. I threw the blankets off myself and rubbed my eyes. As soon as I put my feet on the floor, I remembered why I set the alarm.

Those loud-mouths from Jericho Jr. High needed some schooling.

My heart beat faster the more I thought about it. I love playing soccer more than just about anything. Thinking ahead, I could already smell the sun-warmed grass beneath my cleats.

I got dressed and went downstairs, where the smell of cooking made my stomach rumble. Dad stood by the stove, wearing that silly apron Mom got him for Christmas last year. The one that says *Kiss the Cook.* I could just die of embarrassment on his behalf because Dad thinks it's cool.

"Morning, Sport." Dad's mustachioed face peered over his shoulder at me. "Would you get the OJ out of the fridge?"

"Sure thing, Dad."

I went to retrieve the juice carton, then stopped by the cabinet where we kept our cups and glasses. I spied the table and found that only two places were set.

"Is Mom not eating?"

"She's sleeping in. She had a Zoom call with some partners in China, and she didn't go to bed until a little while ago."

I tried not to let on to Dad how disappointed I was. I prefer Mom's cooking. I'm the only one who does. Everyone else always goes on and on about how much of a gourmet Dad is in the kitchen. He sells insurance. He's not a chef, but he watches so many cooking shows he thinks he is.

The reason I don't like Dad's cooking is how fancy everything has to be. Like, sometimes, I just want pancakes. Just plain old pancakes. Not pancakes with almonds, or grapeseed, or olives, or whatever weird thing he saw on the internet that he wants to try.

I squirmed on my seat as Dad brought the skillet over.

"Banana pancakes this morning, Sport," he said cheerfully.

"Oh thank heav — I mean, thanks, Dad."

Banana pancakes I can deal with.

"You're going to need the energy and the potassium in the pancakes today. That is, if you're going to beat those guys from Jericho."

"We can beat them," I said with determination as I drowned my pancakes in syrup. When they lose all cohesiveness and just fall apart into a spongy mass, that's when I like them. "We just need to give it our all. Those guys from Jericho are a bunch of bragging jerks, but they're pretty good. Daniel, their Center, he's like a tank with a Ferrari engine! The guy never gets tired and he'll plow right over you."

"Isn't that a foul?"

I shook my head.

"Not if you keep your arms tucked in and make contact with the ball, first. Unless the ref decides you used excessive force, or were trying to hurt the other guy."

Dad tries to be interested in what I'm interested in, because he is a pretty good Dad. But sometimes I feel like he has a rare disease that makes him incapable of remembering the rules of soccer.

"See, that concerns me," Dad said after a sip of juice. "You guys don't have anyone to act as a referee. Are there going to be any adults there to supervise?"

I groaned, rolling my eyes so hard I thought they would spin around like a slot machine.

"No, Dad, we don't need adult supervision. It will be fine."

I checked the time and gasped.

"It's already almost nine o'clock? I have to go."

I wolfed down the rest of my meal while my father looked on in concern.

"Slow down, Max. You don't want to give yourself a belly ache, now do you?"

"I'll be fine, Dad, thanks!"

Once I secured my backpack, I grabbed my cleats off the back porch, sending a cloud of dried mud through the air. I would have to remember to sweep it up when I got home, or Mom and Dad would get upset.

I jogged over to my bike and jumped on, pedaling hard. My first stop would be just up the street, four houses down. The bike tires screeched to a halt outside a blue-painted house. I craned my neck, trying to look through the living room curtains to see if I could spot Roberto, our goalie.

The curtains were shut tight. I couldn't see anything. A sound from the side of the house drew my attention. Roberto's yellow cleats appeared, thrust out the side window, followed soon by the rest of his body.

"Hey, Roberto — "

"Shhh!" he put his finger to his lips and sort of ran-tiptoed to where his bike rested against the side of the house. He pushed it out to the street and soon sped ahead of me. I had to hustle to catch up.

"What's up, Roberto? Why are you freaking out?"

He turned his caramel-colored eyes toward me, and he didn't look happy.

"Dude, my Mom found out about that video I posted online."

"The one where you talk about your 'rizz' while dancing in your underwear?"

He hissed through clenched teeth.

"Can you not say that so loud?"

"What's really messed up is that the girl you thought you were talking to online turned out to be Turk from Jericho Junior High."

Roberto got so mad I thought steam would come out of his ears and nostrils. I kind of wanted him fired up, though. The last game we played, Roberto was way too casual and let the other team score on us three times. Three times!

When Roberto's heart was in it, he was a great goalie. I wanted to make sure he felt properly motivated for our match today.

We halted outside of a three story, haunted-house looking place where our friend Jimmy lived. Jimmy usually played

5

wingback, and was almost as stiff a player as Daniel from Jericho.

None of us liked going to his house, though. It freaked us out. His mom and dad were all right, and so was his big brother. It was the house. We all felt certain that there had been a mass murder in there at one point or another. Or maybe a demon summoning seance.

"Go and knock on his door," I said, slapping Roberto on the shoulder.

"What, me? YOU go knock on his door. You're the team captain."

"I'm so not the captain, and I knocked last time."

Roberto sighed.

"Dude, you come up with most of the plays, formations, and strategies, and you're a walking encyclopedia of futbol facts. If you're not the captain, you're as close as we've got."

I couldn't argue with him. Not even when he slapped me on the back.

"So go knock on the door, Muy Capitan!"

I gave him a nasty glare as I made my way through the picket fence gate and up the sidewalk. The upper floor windows stared down at me like the dark eyes of a monster. I swear that when I put my foot on the first step, a chill wind started to blow.

Even though the day was pretty warm, I shivered as I reached up to knock. Just before I touched the door, it flew open, and I yelled.

"What's your problem, dork? Huh-huh, huh-huh."

I looked up at the shaven-headed, broad-faced pain in

the neck known as Jimmy. Living in what looked like a terrifying haunted house never seemed to bother him.

"You scared the crud out of me!"

"I know! I watched you come up the steps, trying not to laugh the whole time. Huh-huh, huh-huh."

"I just hope you're this much of a pain to our opponents," I grumbled.

Jimmy joined us as we moved through the neighborhood, collecting our team. We found our other wingback, Omar, reading comics in his tree house instead of waiting for us with his bike ready to go like he should have been.

Next, we pedaled to the bowling alley and met up with brothers Dallas and Houston McGillicutty, who were our center-back and sweeper. Across the street and around the block from the bowling alley, we joined up with Luis, our holding midfielder.

The mob of us moved on to the next stop. It felt good to be with my team, even if some of them weren't as dedicated as I wished they would be. We met up with Frank, our right winger, just outside the laundromat his family owned.

"That just leaves Mondo and Francois, right?" Jimmy asked. He was asking about our box-to-box and striker.

"They're going to meet us in the park," I said. "They're probably already there since they live right across the street."

"Wait, we're missing somebody," Roberto said, stretching his neck as he did a headcount of our crew. "Um, where's Dennis?"

"Dude, didn't you hear?" Jimmy shook his head, a look of disgust on his freckled face. "Dennis got caught sneaking money out of his mom's purse. He's grounded for the next two weeks."

"Grounded?" Roberto's jaw fell open. "But he's our left winger! It's going to be eleven versus ten!"

"Might as well go home and play video games," Frank said with a sigh.

"Nobody's going home!" I shouted, stepping up onto a retaining wall to get their attention. "Arsenal manager Arsène Wenger said that it's actually harder to beat ten men than eleven."

"Is that true?" Roberto asked.

"Arsenal has the record for most FA cups in history. I think Wenger knows what he's talking about."

Jimmy shrugged his pasty shoulders.

"If Max says it, it's probably true. Besides, we can eat those Jericho Junior High punks for breakfast!"

"Yeah! We can take them!"

I grinned as my team got fired up.

"Now we're ready to play some soccer," I said. "Let's keep this energy all the way to the park. Jericho awaits."

CHAPTER 2

Your Game Is Lame

"I feel like I'm the best, but you're not going to get me to say that."

— Jerry Rice

We came up the last hill to Ike Park and spotted the rival team. Unlike us, they'd chosen to show up in their team uniforms. We weren't supposed to do that. It upset the coaches, something to do with disrespecting the honor of the uniform. Our team fell into hushed silence when we spotted them, and they spotted us. We didn't hate each other or anything. But let's just say the spirit of competition burned pretty bright.

As we approached the Jericho guys, they stopped horsing around. Daniel, their center and sort of team captain, stepped up in front of them. Tall and lean, he usually stood with his head tilted at a weird angle.

Usually, he looked pretty angry, too. Today was no exception.

"You little dweebs ready to get your butts handed to you

on a silver platter?"

Roberto charged forward and snarled.

"Dream on!"

I put my hand on his shoulder and gently pushed him back.

"We'll see what happens, won't we?" I said to Daniel.

He snorted and dug around in his pocket until he came up with a quarter. I approached, ready to make the call.

"Better make sure it's not a double-sided coin, Max," Roberto said.

"We don't need to cheat to beat you Henry Raab Junior High losers," Daniel snapped back. He turned to me, his gaze not quite as angry. "Call it, Max."

"Heads."

He flipped the coin in the air. We all watched as it spun in the morning sunlight, splashing golden light everywhere.

It came down on the back of his hand. Daniel slapped his other hand over it and pulled away after a dramatic pause.

"I told you to check," Roberto groaned.

"It's all good, guys," I replied. "You got the kick off."

We moved onto our side of the pitch. Daniel's team did likewise, except for their kicker, a bushy-headed, wiry kid who could run like the wind: Turk, Roberto's nemesis.

I watched as he prepared to run up on the ball, keeping track of his movements. Would he try to kick it deep into our territory to make us have to cross a greater distance to their goal? Or would he keep the ball close to their side of the pitch, enabling them to get control faster?

He dashed up toward the ball. My eyes narrowed right

before the kick. I saw he was going for the moon.

Turk's cleats made a *whiff* sound as they slashed through the tips of the grass, knocking a few stray blades into the air. His foot smacked the ball with a solid impact. I started running back even before the ball rose into the air.

"Hustle, Jimmy! Hustle!" I cried.

Jimmy stretched his long legs out and intercepted the ball. Turk had kicked the ball so well, it headed right for our goal. Jimmy leaped into the air with a grunt, leaning his head back. He hammered the ball with his forehead, sending it bouncing along the grass.

Dallas intercepted the ball and dribbled it up the field. Four of the Jericho guys streaked toward his position. I sidled along until I was in the right spot.

"Pass!" I shouted.

Dallas faked out the guys coming in on him and then tapped the ball to me. It spun around on its axis like a globe for a dozen feet before I managed to get in front of it.

Dribbling the ball, I moved across the center line and onto their side of the pitch. I squinted as the sun got in my eyes, but I still managed to spot Daniel coming in hard on my left.

He went for the tackle. I waited until the last moment, when he'd fully committed himself to the slide, and then passed the ball to Houston.

"Get him!" Daniel hollered as he slid across the grass, and Houston charged hard at their net. I could already see it was unlikely Houston would penetrate the Jericho defenses. They'd used a 4-4-3 formation, which meant they respected our offense.

"Omar, Jimmy!" I shouted. "Fall back! Jericho is going to get the ball."

Sure enough, one of the Jericho guys tackled the ball right from under Houston. Houston tripped over the back of the other player's calf, tumbling across the grass.

I hoped he would be all right, but I had problems of my own. I ran laterally along beside the Jericho midfielder and their striker, Turk. Turk was one of the few guys on the other team who could run flat out as fast as I could, and he had a head start.

I blinked sweat out of my eyes, legs pumping, heart pounding, as I closed in on him. Turk spotted me coming and started running at an angle.

A couple of my teammates joined me, pressuring Turk. I saw an opportunity for a tackle and ran up to take the ball, only to collide with Mondo. His elbow caught me in the sternum, and my air exploded out of my lungs.

I slammed onto the grass, pain shooting through my back. In an upside-down view, I watched as Turk juked both our fullbacks and got into scoring range.

Turk took his shot. The black and white ball spun with crazy English, making a hissing sound as it rushed toward our net. Roberto leaped, stretching his hand out. His fingertips brushed the edge of the ball, but it spun right on and swooshed into our net.

"Dang it, Roberto," Jimmy moaned.

"The heck with you!" Roberto said. "You let him waltz right past you!"

"Settle down, you two!" I said, getting between them. "It happens. Turk's really darn good. We can get it back."

I stepped between them and pushed them apart. Daniel

wore a cock grin as he leered over at me.

"Your ball," he said mockingly.

I knew he wanted to get a rise out of me. The smart thing would be to not let him, but Daniel was really good at getting under people's skin. I fumed as we placed the ball and prepared for the kickoff. I summoned the guys around for a quick strat session.

"They're piling up most of their guys on their side of the pitch," I said. "They're relying on Daniel and Turk to score their goals for them."

"It worked," Houston grumbled. I was glad to see he was all right.

"Yeah, it worked. Once. Now we know what they're up to, so this is how we're going to play it..."

Frank got set up for the kick after our huddle. He roared like a dinosaur and rushed up to the ball like he wanted to kill it.

Then he just barely tapped the ball, and it skipped a scant three feet over the line.

"Let's go!" I shouted.

Houston, Mondo, Frank, and I sprinted past their defensive line until only one fullback barred our way to the goal. Meanwhile, the rest of our team concentrated on passing and dribbling until they could get the ball to one of the four of us.

Mondo was wide open, so he got the pass. But I saw Daniel coming up fast on his flank. I knew Mondo was tough, but Daniel was like a freight train.

They each kicked opposite sides of the ball, then went down in a tangle of limbs. The ball popped out and bounced a few feet. I raced up and took possession, dribbling toward the enemy goal.

Their fullback went for the tackle, but I twisted in a tight circle and gave him the slip. I had only a split second to line up my shot, but that was all I needed.

I kicked the ball toward the left side of the goal. Their goalie leaped to catch it. My heart sank when his gloved hands slapped on both sides of the ball.

"Toss it, toss it!" Daniel shouted.

The goalie tossed, but Houston and Mondo were all over Daniel. They harried him all the way to our side of the pitch; then Frank got possession of the ball.

We went back and forth for quite a while, neither team scoring a goal, but both of us coming close. As we neared the end of the first half, two things became clear.

One, the Jericho guys were playing to win and weren't going to give up any points without a fight.

Two, our unofficial match had drawn in a gaggle of observers. Usually, we only had a few bored kids watching us, but it looked like someone was having a picnic or family reunion-type deal. I saw coolers, blankets, and truckloads of food.

We reached halftime, and my team gathered by the south side water fountain. While we took turns slaking our thirst, I tried to rally the troops.

"Don't look so dejected, guys. We can still beat them!"

"How?" Frank asked between heavy pants. He looked like he was about to fall over dead. "They won't let us anywhere near their goal."

"Yeah, but they're getting tired. I told you, Jericho Junior High's Coach Stanfield doesn't push cardio enough. Look at them."

It was true that the sweat stains on the other team's clothing were much larger and darker than our own.

"Max is right," Jimmy said. "He knows two things: Eating his boogers and soccer."

"Grow up, Jimmy," Roberto said with a sigh. "But yeah, yeah, they do look tired. Maybe we can beat them."

"Everybody sit down on the grass, try to recuperate," I said.

"Right, let's do it," Jimmy said. "Um, what does recuperate mean?"

"He means take it easy and get our wind back," Roberto replied.

Now that the rest of the team had drunk, I took my turn. I knew that I needed hydration, but I didn't want too much cold water hitting my stomach at once, so I took a sip and waited, took a sip and waited.

A shadow fell over me as I stood at the fountain. I figured it was someone who wanted a drink.

"Sorry," I said without looking, "I'll be done in a second."

"Take your time."

I wiped my mouth and turned to face the man who had spoken. Gray hair and wrinkles marked him as on the older side, but his legs looked like they belonged to a man younger than my dad. From the way he looked at me, I couldn't tell if he was mad or not.

"When you go in for the tackle," he said, "try keeping most of your body over the ball. You're a lot less likely to get knocked down that way."

I gave him a look.

"Um, okay, thanks, mister. Do you play soccer?"

"Not anymore," he replied cryptically. I waited, but he didn't seem to have anything else to say, and the teams were gathering on the field.

"Okay, um, thanks again. Have a good day."

I jogged out to join my guys on the field.

"Who was that guy you were talking to?" Jimmy asked.

"I dunno. Some random grandpa, I guess, but he seems to know something about soccer."

I gave the old man one last look before we prepared for the second half kickoff.

We were down by one, but not for long. Not if I had anything to say about it.

CHAPTER 3

Park the Bus in the Park

"My career was sputtering until I did a 360 and got headed in the right direction."

— Tracy McGrady

"Y ou sure you want to Park the Bus, Max?" Roberto whispered in my ear as we prepared to take the field. "Don't we need to score?"

"We do need goals, but the only way we're going to get them is if we make Jericho run themselves ragged first. Their defense is too tight. If we can gas them out by making them chase us all over the pitch, then we've got it made in the shade."

"I hope you know what you're doing," he grumbled. "Still can't believe I let Turk score on me."

"I told you he got under your skin, dude! That was his whole point from the get-go. Just try to keep your cool...and maybe stay off social media. I think it's your kryptonite."

I slapped him on the shoulder with that zinger and jogged back to midfield. We set ourselves up in a 4-4-2 formation. Mondo was the sole member of our team who dashed to their side of the pitch after kickoff.

The rest of us concentrated on short, fluid passes between us. We focused on keeping the ball more than creating scoring opportunities and made the Jericho guys chase us all over.

It soon became clear Daniel was in the best shape on his team. He was the only one who didn't start to slow down after about ten brutal minutes of our strategy.

Meanwhile, since we were only trying to keep the ball and not score, we were able to dictate the pace and direction of the game. We kept each other from getting worn out with frequent passing and trickery.

When the majority of their team lagged far behind us, I knew it was time to switch it up.

"Blitzball!" I shouted.

Daniel's eyes squinted in confusion as we suddenly switched up our game to a 2-3-5 formation. With five of us pressuring their sole wingback, they didn't stand a chance.

Mondo and Daniel went scrambling for the ball. Daniel slid into a tackle and smacked the ball toward one of his teammates.

Fortunately, Houston was there in the nick of time. He slid and fell on his back but managed to get his foot up and deflect the ball off the side of his cleats. It swung crazily through the air. I jumped up, keeping my arms well out to the sides, and let the ball smack into my chest.

It fell back to the ground and I was already lining up my shot. I gave it everything I had, almost knocking myself over with the power of my kick. The ball spun sideways, tearing a furrow in the grass, shooting for the net.

The Jericho goaltender flopped onto his belly in a vain attempt to stop the goal. Ball met net. I was elated. My team whooped and hollered, slapping me on the back as we trotted back to our side of the pitch.

"GOAL!" Roberto bellowed, cupping his mouth with his hands. "Now that's what I'm talking about!"

"It's even up, but don't get careless! We still have most of the second half to go, and now they'll be ready for us."

Frank jogged up to join our conversation.

"What's the strat, Max? Do we want to park the bus again?"

I surveyed our team. Sweat darkened their clothes, making the garments cling to their bodies.

"No," I said. "We do that, we'll all gas out. It's time for something new."

Even as I spoke the words, I drew a blank on what that strategy should be. Then it hit me — the Jericho guys played a wide midfield game.

"We're going 3-4-3," I said firmly.

"How are we going to score with only two attackers?" Jimmy groaned. "We're going to end up with a tie."

"No, we won't." I stared him down hard. "Jericho is embarrassed. They're going to try really, really hard to get a goal after the kickoff, and we need to concentrate on defense until we get an opening."

I turned and grabbed Houston by the shirt, pulling him in close in case the Jericho guys could read my lips.

"Listen, man, stay on their half of the pitch, no matter

what. Make them forget you exist."

"We're already down one man to their eleven," Houston said, his face turning red. "What if you guys need me?"

"We'll have to make do."

We split up into our formation as Jericho prepared to kick. Turk rocketed the black and white ball down the field until Jimmy intercepted with a head butt. The ball bounced over to me, and I started dribbling toward the enemy pitch.

Daniel and two Jericho players swarmed my position. I looked around frantically, hoping to pass, but they had the field locked up tight. Daniel went in for the tackle but juked me at the last minute. His teammate switched up with me, taking possession of the ball.

I didn't let it get to me. I knew they were going to be aggressive after we scored on them. With eight of our nine outfielders working on defense, we managed to stymie their charge for the goal. Dallas got the ball and made a series of short passes with his brother, working their way to the other half of the pitch.

This was the real nitty-gritty when everyone was tired and achy. My legs felt like they wanted to turn to water, but I ran on, gritting my teeth against the strain. We got within twenty feet of their goal when Jericho got the ball back.

Using their superior numbers, they pressured us hard. We couldn't keep the ball out of our half of the pitch to save our lives. I was starting to worry I'd miscalculated. Just when I was about to signal Houston to come back and help with defense, it happened.

Jericho made a critical error.

Daniel charged at the goal, but our wingbacks were there to cut him off. Turk ran parallel, only about a dozen feet away. All Daniel had to do was pass the ball, and Turk had a pretty darn good shot at scoring on Roberto. Turk had Roberto's number, and we all knew it.

But Daniel messed up. He hogged the ball, deciding he wanted the glory of the winning goal. He took his shot, but Jimmy tackled him, and the ball shot at a slow, arcing angle toward the goal. Roberto easily caught it and tossed it back over to me.

Here we go, I thought. Nothing stood between me and the enemy goal except for their goaltender and a lot of open grass. I dribbled down the field, even as I heard the footfalls of the Jericho team rushing up behind me.

A Jericho player about twice my size charged in like a speeding bullet toward me. He was a fullback, and his cardio wasn't the best. But it didn't have to be, not this time.

I caught Houston out of the corner of my eye. He stood less than ten feet from the goal. I narrowed my gaze and charged hard like I intended to bowl right over my much larger opponent.

I knew it was going to hurt, but I also knew it was going to work.

At the last moment, I switched up my feet and kicked the ball over to Houston. The fullback plowed into me and sent me tumbling head over heels. I think I even saw stars. But as I smacked down hard on my back in the grass, I heard a wonderful sound: the sound of a ball hitting the net.

"Are you all right?"

Dallas helped me to my feet. My back was achy, but I could move, and I could breathe.

"I don't think anything is broken."

I limped back to our side of the pitch. They kicked off, but no sooner than it hit the air our timer went off.

"That's game!" Roberto shouted. "Ha! In your face, Turk!"

"Let's not be sore winners, guys," I said. "Everybody line up for the handshake."

That was the rule. No matter how much we beat each other up on the field, we always shook hands and said good game afterward. Roberto more or less slapped Turk's hand rather than shaking it, but at least it didn't degenerate into a brawl — this time.

"Good game, you little twerp," Daniel said, squeezing my hand almost painfully hard. "It could have gone either way, though."

"Yeah, it could have. Maybe next time you'll get us."

"Count on it."

I made my way over to the line at the water fountain. We were in good spirits since we'd won. Myself, I felt a little bit let down. After looking forward to the soccer game all week, the rest of my weekend just didn't seem as big of a deal.

"Hey, Max," Jimmy said. "You want to come over and play Mortal Street Combat 99?"

Go to the haunted house? No thanks.

"Nah, I've got stuff to do at home. My Dad wants me to help him clean out the garage."

"Your loss, dweeb."

I soon found myself walking out of the park alone. I stopped to scrape the mud off my cleats on a wrought iron fence at the edge of the park when I noticed someone approaching me.

"Hello, Max," said the mystery grandpa I'd spoken with before. "Good game."

"Thanks," I replied. "It was hard there at the end. I didn't know if we would make it."

"It always helps when your opponent makes a mistake," he said, looking down at the park where some of the Jericho guys, Daniel included, were taking turns practicing goal kicks. "That dark-haired boy is good. But he bogarted the ball instead of passing. You didn't make that mistake."

My parents always told me to avoid talking to strangers, but there was something familiar about this guy. I felt like I should know him.

"Um, thanks for the advice, mister, but I need to get home."

"Of course, I don't mean to hold you up. But let me give you something first."

He dug in his pocket and pulled out a beige business card with red and gold lettering across the front. I took it from his wrinkled hands and read the name.

Rex Johnson. Head soccer coach at Caldwell Academy and a living legend. My mouth fell open, and I stared up at him in amazement.

"You're Rex Rocket?"

He cackled, eyes shutting behind his glasses.

"I haven't been called that in a long time, but yes, guilty as charged."

His smile faded, and his face grew serious.

"Max, I've seen a lot of people play this game. I've seen people with more raw natural talent than you possess, but I've never seen anyone with such a keen mind for the game at such a young age. I think you have potential. Real potential."

I stared at the card in my hand. When I spoke, my voice broke.

"You...want me to join Caldwell Academy? Play on the soccer team?"

"Exactly." His smile returned.

"I...I don't know, my parents might not be able to afford it."

"You can get tuition assistance as a student-athlete."

"But Caldwell is two hundred miles away. I'd have to live on campus."

Rex nodded.

"It's a big decision. You should go home and talk it over with your parents. Once you decide, give me a call, even if it's just to say you are not interested."

He turned away and walked back toward his group. Then he stopped and glanced over his shoulder.

"Think about it, Max. This kind of opportunity doesn't come very often. It's best to strike while the iron is hot."

I watched as he rejoined his group at the picnic tables. I stuck the card into my pocket, hefted my cleats, and walked home, so nervous I almost puked up my breakfast.

Me, playing for Caldwell? That was the stuff dreams were made of.

If I could deal with being so far from home.

And if I could get my parents to agree.

24

CHAPTER 4

It's Only a
Couple Hundred Miles

"This year we plan to run and shoot. Next year, we plan to run and score."

— Billy Tubbs

Dad insisted I get in the shower right when I walked in the door. I didn't see a point since we would get all dirty in the garage again anyway, but he said it was to keep germs out of the house.

While I showered, I kept thinking about my meeting with Rex Rocket. Rex had done it all, even playing in the World Cup finals and making himself a legend in the process. If he thought I was good enough for Caldwell Academy, then that was huge.

I joined Dad in the garage. He struggled to drag a huge refrigerator box filled with Christmas decorations across the concrete floor. I went to the other side and helped push.

"There he is," Dad said. "I bet we can knock this out in under an hour if we apply some stick-toit-tivness."

"Yeah, it's important to apply yourself to things you find important," I replied.

Dad stopped, turning a frown my way.

"Is something wrong, Max? You seem a little distracted. I thought you won your game?"

"We did. It's what happened after that has me all weirded out."

Dad put his hands on his hips.

"Did someone try to bully you at the park?"

"No," I said.

"Did they try to get you to drink beer or do illicit substances?"

I groaned and rolled my eyes.

"No, that's not it at all. It wasn't anything bad."

Dad stroked his chin while he stared at me. A fly buzzed around his head, and he absent-mindedly swatted it away before speaking.

"It wasn't anything bad, you say, but I can tell you're upset. It's okay to talk to me, Max. You know you can come to me and your mother with anything, right?"

I hissed through my teeth.

"Can I, though?"

Dad's eyes got that stern look.

"Out with it, kiddo. I'm going to have an anxiety attack if you don't tell me what's going on."

I took a deep breath, and rushed through the whole spiel before I lost my nerve.

"I met Rex Rocket at the park, and he coaches at Caldwell Academy, and he wants me to join his team, but it's 200 miles away, and I'd have to live on campus, and I'm afraid you and Mom won't let me go if I decide I want to."

Dad stood there for a long moment, blinking slowly. He sighed and took off his glasses, rubbing the bridge of his nose.

"Rex Rocket...you mean Reginald Johnson?"

"Yeah. He's a coach now, and he says I have potential."

Dad blew air out of his lips, making his hair dance. I could tell he was worried.

"Max, this is a huge decision. You'd be a long way from home, and your mother and I wouldn't be there, in the same house, to help you."

"Yeah, I know."

"Don't blow this off, Max. It's important."

Frustration bubbled up out of me.

"I know it's important! I know it's going to be rough, being away from my family, and my friends. I know I'll have to give up having my own room and probably will have lots more rules I have to follow."

Dad's eyes softened.

"Max, do you want to go?"

"Yes...no...I don't know!" I threw my hands up in the air. "I guess I need to think about it more. But will you and Mom let me? That's what I'm worried about."

Dad picked up a box of nuts and bolts and slapped it onto the workbench. He left his hand on the box as he turned to look at me.

"I think that if you want to go, it's our job as parents to support you — "

I gasped, my heart racing in my chest.

"Calm down, Max. We still need to discuss this with your mother. She should be done with tutoring soon. We can talk about it then."

I nodded, working my jaw silently. Leaving my home, my neighborhood, where I'd lived my entire life...that was going to be a huge step.

If I decided to go to Caldwell.

But Dad was right. There was no point in worrying about it until we talked to Mom. If she said no, I knew that Dad would go along with her. Maybe because Mom was a teacher, Dad usually listened to her side of things.

I really hoped she would say yes. Even if I decided against going to Caldwell, I wanted to have the option. I guess I wanted it to be my decision.

Dad and I finished cleaning up the garage. It only took us about an hour because we didn't spend much time talking. We just worked in silence. Dad would stop and look at me sometimes, though, and act kind of sad. I knew he would miss me. I'd miss him and Mom, too, not to mention Roberto, and Houston, and all the other guys. Even Freddy, who was kind of a pain. I'd miss him too.

I think Dad wanted her to say yes, though. When she finished tutoring, he suggested we eat at her favorite Italian restaurant. My Mom has a thing for toasted ravioli. Dad even made me go put on a nice shirt to wear to the restaurant, and Mom wore a dress for the first time in ages.

Dad and I were on our best behavior. Mom acted like it was all perfectly normal until the cannoli came out for dessert. I no sooner crunched into chocolatey goodness when Mom arched her brows and spoke.

"So, what are you two trying to butter me up for?"

I gave a panicked look at Dad. He shrugged in so fake-casual a way I wanted to roll my eyes.

"What makes you say that, honey?"

Mom laughed and took a sip of her wine before swirling it around in the glass.

"Please, Ted. You took me to Valabar's, you put on cologne, and Max is wearing a collared shirt. Just tell me what's up."

Dad and I looked at each other. I waited, but he didn't say anything to Mom. I knew he wanted me to do it.

I set the remaining half of my cannoli down and washed my mouth out with milk to buy myself time.

"Um," I said intelligently. "I met Rex Rocket...I mean, Reginald Johnson at the park today, and he wants me to play for Caldwell Academy."

Mom blinked in confusion.

"Who's Reginald Johnson? And what does he have to do with that overpriced, elitist school?"

My heart sank. I knew Mom, being a teacher in a public school, wouldn't be thrilled with the idea of me going to a private academy. I just didn't know she was going to be this bad about it.

"Rex Johnson is a legendary soccer player, Maria," Dad said. "He coaches for the Academy, and apparently, he saw Max play today and was impressed enough to offer him a spot on the team."

Mom shook her head, face twisting up into a frown.

"No. It's too far away."

"Mom!"

"Shh," Dad said, putting his finger to his lips. "We're in public, keep your voice at a respectful level."

"Mom," I said a lot quieter, "it's not that far away. You can drive there in a couple of hours."

Mom gave me a glare that made me squirm in my seat.

"I do not want to raise my son long-distance! Why can't Max just play soccer for the school here in town? They're a good team."

"Yeah, but Mom, the academy has a GREAT team," I said, trying not to sound whiny. "If I play for Caldwell, it will really make me stand out from the pack."

"Caldwell can give Max the tools he needs to reach the professional ranks," Dad said softly.

Mom put her fork down, seeming quite upset. Now, I felt guilty for making her sad.

"Max is only twelve! Does he have to go away to school already?"

"Mom, please," I said.

Mom pushed her chair back and stood up.

"I was supposed to get six more years with my son before he left me forever!"

Mom stormed out of the restaurant. I looked at Dad in shock. How could the evening have gone any worse?

"She's not going to let me," I said. I wasn't sure how to feel. Part of me was relieved. I mean, I didn't want to move away from home. The prospect scared the crud out of me worse than watching every movie about ghosts combined.

But I still wanted the decision to be mine. If Mom said no, then I was done for.

"Let me talk to her, champ," Dad said, motioning the waiter over. "I'd like the check, please."

I sighed, wondering if Dad could really talk Mom down. It had happened before, but not very often. As Dad handed over his credit card, I looked out the big picture window to see my Mom standing on the sidewalk outside the restaurant. She seemed really upset.

"Maybe I shouldn't have asked," I said, feeling more guilty than ever. "I mean, Mom's right. I can play for the school team."

Dad shook his head.

"The school team here doesn't travel outside the county. If you want to become a star player and get drafted to a great team, you'll need to play on a travel team. The academy can do that for you."

"Yeah, but look at Mom! How am I supposed to concentrate on playing soccer when I know she's at home feeling sad because I'm gone?"

Dad smiled and mussed up my hair.

"You're a good kid, Max. You've got a good heart. It's fine to make sacrifices for someone else's happiness. It's noble, even..."

His expression grew more serious.

"But that doesn't mean you should suppress your own dreams just because it might make someone else uncomfortable if you don't. Max, you were born to be a pro soccer player. I really believe that."

I perked up and smiled, feeling all warm on the inside.

"Thanks, Dad."

I looked out the window and saw Mom, and all of a sudden, the good feeling wasn't so good anymore.

"But what about Mom?"

"She'll understand, Max," Dad said, his voice steady. "She wants you to follow your dreams just as much as I do."

"Yeah, but...I don't know if I want to convince her now. It makes me feel bad."

Dad gave me a long, hard look. I shifted in my chair under his gaze.

"Max, it's good that you feel empathy for your mother. It really is. But if you don't go to Caldwell, you're going to regret it for the rest of your life."

I gave him a look.

"How do you know?"

Dad looked over at Mom and sighed.

"A long time ago, when I wasn't much older than you — "

"Like in the Jurassic period?"

"Ha ha." Dad waited a moment, I guess, to see if I was done making jokes. I was. "When I was about your age, I won a lot of angling championships."

"What's angling?"

"It's a fancy word for fishing."

I gasped and pointed at him.

"All those trophies in the garage, the ones with the fish on them. Those are yours?"

He nodded.

"I was pretty good. Maybe not as good as you are at soccer, but I got offered an apprenticeship with a pro. The only problem was it would take me away all summer."

"Why is that a problem?"

He paused for a moment before speaking again. I think he was remembering way, way back.

"Do you remember when Grandma and Grandpa had that corner store downtown?"

"Yeah, barely. I was a zygote back then."

He chuckled.

"It used to be that I spent my summers working in the corner store. Weekends, too. My parents...your grandparents, they guilted me into turning down the opportunity so I could help out with the store."

"Oh, man. I'm sorry, Dad."

"Don't be. It was my decision, and I met your mother working in that store, so it all turned out okay." His eyes got kind of sad. "Still, I always wonder what might have been if I had said yes to that apprenticeship."

The table got quiet. I cleared my throat before speaking.

"Hey, Dad?"

"Yes?"

"Is that why you don't display your angling trophies in the house? Because they make you kind of sad?"

Dad arched his eyebrows.

"Yes, I think so. But maybe it's time we moved them into the house."

He left a tip on the table and stood up.

"Come on. Let's go home. Your Mom and I have some things to discuss, but don't worry. She'll come around."

"What makes you so sure, Dad?"

"Because she loves you. Just as much as I do."

I felt my eyes get all hot and squinty like they do right before I cry. I hate crying in public. I ran up and hugged my Dad tight, burying my face in his chest so no one could see.

CHAPTER 5

Home Is Where the Hurt Is

"Nobody in football should be called a genius. A genius is a guy like Norman Einstein."

— Joe Theissman

Man, the ride home sure was uncomfortable. It felt like we were all boxers who had gone to their neutral corners between rounds. Mom didn't talk, and neither did Dad. I was afraid to say anything, either, and break the truce.

When we got home, Mom and Dad went out into the backyard and sat in the gazebo. They did that a lot when they wanted to talk and didn't want me to hear them. I tried watching them for a while, but Dad turned toward me, and I had to duck down beneath the window in my bedroom.

I had to get my mind off it, so I turned on my console and picked up my controller. I had to slap the controller a couple of times to get the red light to stay on. Once I connected to the net, I found a huge list of messages waiting for me.

"Everybody wants some," I mumbled to myself as I sought out an opponent online. I had my customized Barcelona FC 2020 team ready to rumble.

I didn't bother putting on a headset. I wasn't in the mood for trash talk tonight. Mainly, I wanted to try out some new strategies knocking around inside of my head. The game against Jericho had been close, much too close.

I experimented with a High Press tactic, trying to keep all my players on the opposite end of the pitch. I hoped to pressure the other player, and keep him scrambling on the defensive. Also, with all of my players up near their goal, I hoped to create more scoring opportunities.

Things were going pretty good until my opponent got control of the ball and ran it back to my half of the pitch. I sucked in air through my teeth as the striker scored a goal.

Frustrated, I switched things up. I focused on counter attacks and wound up getting a goal after a high-pressure play.

Time ran out on the clock, leaving the game a draw. I set the controller down, my mind spiraling as it went over every play of the game. Some things didn't translate to the real world. For example, my video game teammates rarely missed passes or shifted out of their preassigned positions to take on other roles.

But the basic formations and strategy sure as heck translated to the real world. I thought that maybe I could make better use of the High Press in real life. I was so lost in thought I forgot all about my Mom and Dad until I heard a knock at the door.

"Come in," I said.

Mom pushed open the door, and the second I saw her kind of sad smile, I knew what decision had been made. I ran to her and hugged her tight.

"I'm sorry, Mom," I said, trying not to cry. "I know you're going to miss me, and I'm going to miss you."

"Oh, hush," she said with a chuckle, stroking my hair. It felt really nice when she did that. "I'm going to be fine, and so are you. You know why?"

I pulled back from her, and our eyes met. I shook my head no.

"Because you're going to video call me three times a week: Monday, Wednesday, and Friday. Are we clear?"

"Yes, ma'am," I said.

"Not only that, but when I text you, you're going to answer it as soon as humanly possible. I'm going to have your schedule, so I'll know when you're playing a game or in the middle of a class. Don't put me off, or I'll pull you out of Caldwell Academy so fast it will make your head spin."

"Yes, ma'am," I said again.

She gave me a long, stern look, I guess to make sure it had sunk in. Then she hugged me tighter than ever.

"Oh, Maxwell...you're going to be great. And Coach Johnson seems like a nice man."

I gasped and looked up at her.

"You've talked to him?"

She grinned.

"Of course I talked to him. Right after your father and I discussed the academy, I thought it would be prudent to speak with Rex the Rocket."

"It's just Rex Rocket, Mom. Not Rex the Rocket."

She laughed and kissed me on top of my head.

"Just remember, the Academy is a school first. You have to keep at least a B average, or they won't let you play on the team."

"You know I get good grades, Mom."

Mom pursed her lips into a frown.

"Yes, you do get good grades, but the Academy is going to be a lot more competitive than Henry Raab. You'll have to work harder than ever. Those other kids are going to be getting pushed by their parents to excel."

Now, I was starting to get worried. I had been so excited about the soccer part of the academy that I hadn't really thought much about the schooling. I always did well in school, turned in my homework on time, and passed my tests.

"Don't look so worried, Max," Mom said, kissing my head again. "You'll do fine as long as you put in the effort."

"I guess it's like when Messi first went from a regional to a national club. He had to adjust to a more competitive environment, too."

"Then be like Messi and adapt."

She hugged me one more time, then went back into the hallway.

"Don't stay up too late," she said before closing the door with a click.

I flopped onto my bed and stared up at the ceiling. A giddy laugh started in my chest and bubbled up out of my mouth. She said yes! I was going to Caldwell Academy.

But the downside was that I was going to Caldwell

Academy. I wouldn't get to see my friends except on some weekends and holidays.

And I was going to have to study, study, study. Harder than ever before. Not to mention, the other kids on the soccer team would be the best their neighborhoods had to offer, too.

After that weekend, I had three weeks to wait until Caldwell started its new semester. Three weeks of torture. I felt like I wanted to just get on my bike and ride all the way to the academy, just to get it over with.

But as the day I was going to leave got closer and closer, I started to freak out. It didn't help much when Roberto and Jimmy tried to scare me out of going to the academy.

"You're going to have a roommate, you know," Roberto said while we hung out in his backyard, taking turns kicking the ball into his garage.

"Yeah, I know."

"What if you don't like your roommate? What if they're a big jerk, or their breath smells like old cheese?"

I gave him a dirty look.

"Come on, Roberto. You don't know any of that."

"Yeah, I do. My cousin went to Caldwell Academy and he says that they always give the new guy the crazy weirdo for a roommate. He also says they only have wheat bread and white milk in the cafeteria."

I did my best to ignore him. But the next day, when Jimmy and I were biking to the comic book store, he let me have it.

"Dude," Jimmy said as we pedaled down main street. "All those kids at Caldwell are gonna be rich. None of them are going to want to be friends with the poor kid."

"Shut up, Jimmy. And I'm not poor."

"Does your family own a private jet?"

"No, of course not."

"Then, as far as the Caldwell brats are concerned, you're poor. Everyone is going to hate you."

I slammed down on the brakes, leaving a streak of rubber behind me as I ground to a halt. Jimmy pedaled another dozen feet before he realized I'd stopped.

"Stop it, Jimmy," I said. "I'm freaked out enough without you acting like a big jerk about it."

"You think I'm a jerk, just wait until you meet your new classmates."

"Why are you doing this, man? I thought you were my friend."

I pedaled away from him, racing up the hill and leaving him in my dust. When he finally caught up, I was sitting on my bike outside the comic book store, feeling pretty upset.

"Dude." Jimmy sighed. "I just don't want you to leave. Sorry, I'm being a jerk about it, all right? That's probably why 'Berto and the guys have been giving you the business, too."

"Yeah, well...sorry, I have to leave."

Jimmy snickered.

"Don't be too sorry. With you gone, I just became the star player on our team."

We laughed, then went into the store. I tried to memorize everything in the shop because I wouldn't be coming here once a week as I had since I was seven. I'd either have to order comics online or hope that Caldwell Academy had a shop in biking distance.

The last weekend before the semester started, my parents threw me a going away party. Everyone on the team showed up, which was pretty cool. We had fried chicken, and ice cream cake, and a pinata, almost like it was my birthday.

When the party was over and we were cleaning up, Mom came over to me, her hands behind her back.

"Hey, Max. Your father and I got something for you. Think of it as a going away present."

She pulled a gold-foil-wrapped box from behind her back and placed it in my hands.

"Aw, you shouldn't have."

I don't know why adults always say that when they get a present any other time than the holidays, but it just kinda popped out of my mouth. I already knew what was inside. At least, I thought I did, just by the weight.

"Go ahead, open it."

Mom stood there with her eyes all sparkly like a Christmas tree. I realized that this present really meant a lot to her. I decided to act all super excited no matter what turned out to be inside, just to make her happy.

The gold foil wrapping crinkled and ripped as I opened the gift. When I saw the famous lightning bolt and hammer logo, my heart thudded in my chest like crazy. Had my parents really dropped a bunch of money on Valhallans?

I didn't even dare to breathe as I lifted the lid from the box. The smell of new leather and rubber hit my nostrils. I'd smelled that same smell many times before, and it was always a good one.

Metallic gold cleats gleamed inside the box. I felt light-headed and dizzy. Valhallan Baldurdash. The best cleat Valhallan manufactured.

"Mom, this is...this is too much, I don't know..."

"Breathe, Maxwell," she said, putting her arm around my shoulder. "Go ahead, try them on."

"But Mom, these must have cost a lot of money."

"I've been tutoring on the weekends, and I'm a master-level teacher, honey. You let me worry about money. You need to worry about academics and soccer. And trying on these sick new kicks."

I laughed and settled down on the sofa to try them on.

"I can't believe I have a pair of Baldurdash on my feet. My feet. It's just the best, Mom. Thank you."

"You're welcome, honey. I just know you're going to do great things at Caldwell Academy."

I just had to wear my new cleats and jog around the neighborhood a few times. It kind of made me sad, though, seeing all the things I would leave behind when I went to the academy.

I mean, there's the treehouse I built with Roberto and the skating rink where Jimmy and I had the hot dog eating contest — we both lost when we hurled — and how can I forget the park, where we played so many games of soccer?

I finished my run in our backyard, where it all began. I stood in the same spot I had all those years ago when I kicked my first futbol into the garage wall.

"I'm gonna miss this place," I whispered.

I went inside because I felt tired after the party and

my run. I slept for like twelve hours. The next weekend, my Dad and I drove up to the academy. We spent a good hour of the trip at a truck stop, playing one of those claw games so Dad could get a Sailor Moon Lunar Scout doll for his collection.

Took us a hundred dollars, but he got the darn thing.

With his scout doll secured to the rearview mirror, we continued on our journey to Caldwell. The closer we got, the more I felt like a bundle of fireworks about to go off. Dad noticed.

"Are you all right, Max?"

"Yeah. I'm fine."

"You're acting anxious."

I stared out the window as the landscape blurred past.

"I'm happy, Dad. But I'm also kind of sad, and kind of scared. Is that normal?"

Dad laughed his full-throated, hyena laugh he reserves for special occasions.

"Oh, Max, it's so normal. It's so normal. If you weren't feeling this way, I would be worried."

We started up a hill, and the woods got closer to the road.

"I think we're getting close," Dad said.

We passed a sign that read *Caldwell Academy 1 Mile*. My heartbeat got so fast I thought for sure my chest would burst open like in those Alien movies. The road changed. Like, one minute it was the usual gray pavement, and all of a sudden we were on a road so black it was almost scary.

"Feel that smooth ride?" Dad asked with a grin. "This is a very nicely made road."

He wasn't kidding. The yellow lines stood out like lightning bolts against that sheer black. And the lines, they didn't have so much as a smudge of dirt on them. No tire marks, either.

When we reached the top of the hill, the woods retreated again, and we got a good look at the campus for the first time. I mean, we'd seen it online and in virtual tours, but this was different.

"It's...so big," I whispered.

"Yes, isn't it great? They have everything here you could possibly need. Gymnasium, commissary, biking trails, Frisbee, golf courses, everything."

Caldwell Academy had a four-year program: Grades six through nine. I was coming in at the bottom, a Frosh. Froshes were the lowest of the low, the first year students who everyone else looked down on. This meant most of the other students I saw were both older and larger than me.

I felt like a little kid. All of a sudden I wanted to crawl back into the car and run back home. But I didn't. Because when I looked over at the stadium — yes, stadium — where the Caldwell Cannons played, I knew I was right where I needed to be.

It would be the first time I got to play in an actual stadium, and I was super, super hyped. It made up for the fear. It made up for everything.

My path to the professional leagues started here at Caldwell.

"Let's get you checked into your dorm."

Dad got us lost real quick. The academy had its own road system, and it was all one way. This meant when Dad missed a turn...which he did. A lot...we wound up having to go all the way around.

Not only was this annoying but, the other students were starting to notice we kept making circles around the campus.

"Dad, come on! If you were Indiana Jones, the Nazis would have gotten the Ark."

"Take it easy, Sport, I finally figured it out. This is where we need to turn."

We pulled off the road and into a parking lot in front of two big buildings with lots of windows. A sign outside said *Artemis Residence Halls A and B.*

"See?" Dad said proudly as he parked near the entrance. "I told you I knew where I was going."

I got out of the car and ran to the hatchback. I had to get my stuff out before Dad did something to embarrass me further.

By the time Dad got out of his seatbelt and opened the car door, I was already jogging for the two buildings. I figured there would be a check-in desk or something to tell me how to find my dorm room.

"I've got the first load, Dad," I shouted as I ran past.

Dad didn't have time to reply. I stopped running when I reached the end of the parking lot. The two residence halls shared a green space between them, like a miniature park. I spotted a soccer ball sitting near the sidewalk that ran around the grassy area.

So, I figured, why not? I kicked it into the goal about twenty feet away without even putting down my luggage.

I grinned because it had been a pretty good kick, especially considering I had all that extra weight on me.

"What are you doing?"

I nearly jumped out of my skin. I turned around to find a girl about my age glaring at me. I looked at her, then the ball, and felt bad.

"I'm sorry," I said. "I didn't know that was your ball. I shouldn't have played with something that didn't belong to me."

She shook her head, cocking one black eyebrow.

"I don't care that you kicked my ball. It's a soccer ball, homes. You're supposed to kick it. I mean, what are you doing in the girls dorms?"

CHAPTER 6
Sugar and Spice and Not So Nice

"Better to remain silent and be thought a fool than to speak out and remove all doubt."

— Abraham Lincoln

I stood there like an idiot for a long time before I really processed what she'd said.

"The...girl's dorms?"

I didn't know if I was more embarrassed or angry.

"Darn it, Dad, you got us so lost I wound up at the wrong dorms! Listen, what's your name?"

"Augusta Lorena Sanchez Villa-Lobos Ramirez."

"Um, yeah...listen, um..."

"Everybody calls me Lobo."

"Right. Ms. Lobo, I'd really appreciate it if you didn't tell anyone about this — "

Of course, right then, about a dozen more girls came out of the dorms, along with an adult I took to be a teacher or an RA. They flocked over to us and surrounded Lobo and me before I could even think straight.

"Hi, Lobo, who's your new friend? She has really short hair."

"She is a he," Lobo said.

"What?"

The adult woman came over to me, a confused frown on her face. I took her to be about ten years older than my Dad, and from the looks of her, she didn't smile very often.

"Young man, what do you think you are doing? You can't just creep around the girl's dorms."

"Creep around?" I sputtered. "I'm not creeping! I didn't know these were the girl's dorms, all right?"

"Max, there you are!"

My Dad came up, dragging the rest of my stuff along behind him in a cart.

"I made sure to grab your snoogie," he said, tossing a baby blanket I hadn't used since I was five. "Your mother insisted I not forget."

The girls all snickered at me as I rushed over to my father.

"Dad, shut up! This is the wrong dorm. I need to get to the boy's dorm before you make me a laughingstock."

"Oh. I think it's too late for that, homes," Lobo said, laughing hardest of all.

We left in humiliated defeat. We soon found ourselves at Apollo Residence Halls one and two. The boys' dorm.

"I'm going to be a social outcast on my first day," I groaned as we pulled up. A few other students glanced our way but quickly went back to their conversations. Dad and I weren't the only people moving in for the start of the semester. I hoped that meant I could blend in.

"Max, we're all the way on the other side of campus. No way has word traveled this fast. Besides, there has to be more interesting stuff than someone mistakenly showing up at the wrong dorm going on."

I sighed.

"Maybe you're right, Dad."

I dragged my bags along behind me, rolling across the sidewalk. We passed by the first group of students without incident. Most of them were upperclassmen, so I basically didn't exist to them.

But the next gaggle of students was closer to my age. A short, red-haired boy suddenly pointed at me as we passed.

"Hey, it's Mr. Snoogie."

The kids all laughed. I wanted to die. The red-haired kid held up his phone so I could see the screen and pushed play. A video, clearly shot on a cell phone, started playing.

I realized it was a short vid of my Dad coming up to give me my old blankie. One of the girls had filmed it and posted it on the internet.

"Well, I guess that's going to be my nickname," I said with a sigh of resignation. "Thanks, Dad. I didn't need friends or anything here."

"Don't be so dramatic, Max. Once they get it out of their system, they'll find someone else to tease."

We entered the residence hall. I was in awe at the marble

floors and the polished woodwork. Statues and suits of armor lined the support columns holding up the arched lobby ceiling. The place looked as super fancy as it was.

"Wow, would you look at this place?" Dad said, gawking like a tourist. I didn't even care anymore. I was already filled up on embarrassment.

Dad found his way to the reception desk. A helpful old man sitting there told us how to get to the second floor, west wing, where my room was.

My roommate didn't seem to be home. I was worried he might turn out to be a jerk, or have breath that smelled like cheese. I would have to wait to find out, though.

Dad helped me unpack. There wasn't a lot to the dorm room. We had a mini fridge, two computer desks, and a door that led to the bathroom. Other than our bunk beds, that was it. Clearly, my roommate had chosen the bottom bunk because his stuff was sitting there.

I wanted the top bunk anyway, so it didn't bother me.

"I wonder who my roommate is."

Dad zipped up my now empty suitcase and stored it in the closet before he replied.

"I don't know, but whoever he is, he has good taste in music."

I looked at all the rock and roll posters on the wall and sighed.

"You would think so. You don't like any music that was made this century."

"That's because it's all beeps and boops."

He mussed my hair, and we laughed. Then I hugged him

so tight I nearly cracked his spine.

"Do you have your class schedule?"

"Yes," I mumbled into his stomach.

"What about your soccer practice?"

"We meet on the field tomorrow morning at eight for tryouts."

"I'm sure you'll do great."

Dad squeezed my shoulder, then turned to leave.

"If you need anything, day or night, call us, okay? Even if you're just scared."

"Dad, geez, I'm twelve, I'm not five. I've been on overnight trips with the scouts before."

"Yes, but this is different. I love you, Max. Good luck tomorrow."

"Thanks."

I walked Dad down to the car. We hugged again, and then he left. I watched until I couldn't see his tail lights any longer and then went back inside.

I wanted to explore campus, but the thought of being called Mr. Snoogie kept me from doing that. Instead, I got out my phone and watched highlights from last year's World Cup.

I guess I got pretty lost in that. I'd watched it before, of course, but on the third or fourth time through, I really picked up on a lot of new stuff. I wanted to be one of those guys, playing on the grandest stage of them all, for the biggest prize of all.

The door shutting startled me. I looked over to see a kid

my age with dirty, dishwater blonde hair and an amused smile standing just inside the room. His nose was slightly upturned, and a dusting of light freckles coated his cheeks and forehead. An easy smile tugged the corners of his wide mouth.

"You must be my roomie," he said. "Max, right?"

I slid off the bunk bed and went over to shake his hand because Mom had insisted that I do that when I met my roommate. She made me pinky swear and everything.

"Yes, nice to meet you. You're Nigel, right?"

"Yeah. Nice to meet you, too. So, what were you watching so intently when I came in? A dirty movie?"

"What?" I sputtered. "No! Even if I wanted to be gross, my parents can see everything I do on my phone. I was watching the World Cup."

"World Cup? Is that hockey?"

"Um, no, it's Soccer."

"Oh."

His eyes widened.

"Oh! Yeah, okay, I get it now. You're that poor kid Rex Rocket handpicked for his junior varsity squad."

My heart sank.

"I'm not exactly poor."

Nigel shrugged.

"I don't mean nothing by it. Just saying, you must be really, really freaking good at soccer. I don't play sports, myself. I'm a musician."

"I could never tell."

I looked at the posters, and we both laughed.

"So, what do you think of Caldwell so far?" he asked.

"Um, I haven't seen much of it, not yet. I just moved in today."

"Yeah, I've been here all break. My Dad has a new girlfriend, and they need space or something like that. It's all good with me. I've already made a lot of connections here."

"Connections?"

"Yeah, connections." He winked. "You ain't gonna get nowhere at Caldwell without connections. Speaking of which, you want to come out and hang with some of my friends tonight? We're going to have a bonfire out in the woods."

"That sounds so cool, but I have to get up super early. Soccer tryouts are tomorrow."

He shook his head.

"You don't need to worry. Everybody knows that the soccer team is preordained based on legacies."

"Legacies? What are legacies?"

Nigel rolled his eyes and sighed.

"See, this is what I mean when I say you're one of the poor kids."

He put his arm on my shoulder and walked me over to the window.

"Take a look out there, Max. What do you see?"

"Um, the campus? A bird taking a dump on someone's windshield?"

He laughed.

"I like you, Max. No, I mean, look at the names on the buildings. Those are the same names that have been there like, forever. The same families keep sending their spoiled brats — myself included — to this Academy. If a Legacy wants to play soccer, by god, they're going to make the team. Tryouts be damned."

I felt a stroke of panic.

"Wait, I'm not a legacy. Do you think I can still make the team?"

"Ah, sure. It's in the bag. You were handpicked, after all. Of course, if I were you, I'd be freaking out even more."

"Why is that?"

He slapped me on the back and smiled.

"Because everybody knows you were handpicked. So you better be super freaking good at those tryouts, because everyone will expect you to be."

He grabbed his phone off the charger and left.

"No pressure!" he said just as the door shut.

I sighed and flopped down into a chair.

"No pressure. Yeah, right."

CHAPTER 7

People are Strange When You're a Stranger

"Follow me, boys, I feel lucky!"

— General George Custer

I probably should have gone to the bonfire because I didn't sleep a darn wink most of the night.

It was all strange, new, and different. I looked up at an unfamiliar ceiling when I laid on the top bunk. I began to feel just how far away my favorite places were now.

I remember thinking *this is it. This is for real.*

Caldwell Academy had one of the most elite youth soccer programs in the entire country, maybe even the entire world. A who's who list of soccer stars came out of Caldwell, having played at Cannon Stadium before moving on to college and professional leagues.

I wanted to be one of them. I wanted to be a champion.

I wanted to be the next Messi.

When my alarm went off, I was already awake. I got out of bed and put on my gear, save for my Valhallas. Those I would not put on until I reached the stadium field.

I fell in with a group of other Frosh, lining up at the cafeteria. It seemed like I wasn't the only one who'd had trouble sleeping.

"I guess I wasn't the only one staring at an unfamiliar ceiling last night," I muttered to myself.

"What's that, Mr. Snoogie?"

I groaned and turned around to face Lobo. She had her arms crossed over her chest and wore a mean smile.

"What are you doing up? Aren't vampires afraid of the sun?"

"You're funny, Mr. Snoogie," she said without missing a beat. "You should take that act on the road. And leave it there."

A couple of other kids went, "ooooh." All of a sudden, a lot of eyes were on us. She'd just zinged me good. I wanted to get her back.

"Oh yeah, well, the alphabet called, Augusta Lorena Sanchez Villa-Lobos Ramirez. It wants its letters back."

Her eyes widened, and her mouth fell open. I mentally declared victory, and they opened the doors to the cafeteria right about then, so she didn't have a chance for a comeback.

The smell of sausage, biscuits, and gravy filled the air. My belly growled. I was happy to see it was a buffet-style setup. That meant I could choose my own food. I got some melon slices and biscuits and gravy. I knew the carbs in the biscuits would help fuel me during the tryouts.

I looked for a place to sit. No one seemed inviting. Everyone acted like they knew each other already, sitting together, laughing, and talking.

Unsure of what to do, I wound up sitting all by myself at a table at the end of the cafeteria. I felt really lonely. I was used to eating meals with my family or my classmates back at Henry Raab.

The food tasted good, though. I had to say that for Caldwell Academy.

When I finished up, I took the long way from the cafeteria to the stadium. The main academic buildings formed a sort of X shape in the center of campus. You had the Arts and Music building, the Language Arts and Linguistics building, the Mathematics building, and the History and Social Studies building.

As a Frosh, I would be attending classes at all four buildings. Next year, I would pick a concentration area to focus on.

If I made it to next year. I had to ace these tryouts, or I would be going home. I couldn't imagine going back to face my friends as a failure.

"Buck up, little trooper," I muttered to myself as I approached the stadium. "You can do this. Rex Rocket himself said you had potential. That's like Batman saying you're good at fighting crime."

I walked around the stadium until I found the entrance tunnel. Once I entered the cool, concrete darkness, I felt a shiver go down my spine. I got my first glimpse at the pristine emerald green field and the stark white pitch lines.

When I stepped out of the tunnel, I stopped to put on my new cleats. As I stood up, I nearly collided with another student.

"I'm sorry," I said, looking up into the face of...Daniel?

"Oh, it's you," Daniel said with a snort. "Just stay out of my way, and we won't have any problems."

He pushed past me to join the other potential players. My jaw fell open when I saw how many people were trying out. There must have been around sixty or more.

I wondered how many were legacies. Did I even have a chance of making the team?

Even if they weren't legacies, these guys were good. I mean, real good. I knew that competing against them would be a challenge. That didn't mean I was going to give up.

I started stretching because I knew that any tryout run by Rex Rocket was going to be rough. It wasn't long before a shrill whistle split the air. We all turned to see Rex Rocket walking out to the middle of the field.

"All right, listen up," he bellowed. "For those of you who don't know me, my name is Coach Johnson. Not Rex Rocket, Coach Rocket, Coach Rex, or any other combination of coach, Rocket, or Rex I have not covered."

He stared us down from behind his sunglasses for a long moment, I guess to let it sink in.

"And for those of you who DO know me," Coach said, smiling out of nowhere. "You know I'm going to make you suffer on this tryout, and you showed up anyway. Congratulations."

Coach motioned over two other men.

"These are my assistant coaches, Bobby and Stan. Bobby is the one with the mustache. You might recognize both of them from when they played in international leagues. These guys are legit, and if you listen to them, they can help you a lot."

Coach looked us over and then shook his head as if unimpressed.

"All right, first things first, we're going to do a light little warm-up."

His face twisted into a grotesque mask, and he blasted on that whistle.

"Now drop and give me twenty push-ups."

"What is this, the army?" Daniel griped.

"What was that?" Coach snapped.

"Nothing," Daniel said, looking worried.

Coach got right up in his face.

"What did you say, son? Did you say that we should do thirty push-ups instead of twenty? I agree!"

He looked over at the rest of us.

"Thanks to Daniel here, you can all drop and give me thirty."

I dropped to the sun-warmed grass. I didn't do a lot of push-ups outside of PE class. When I got to fifteen, I started breathing hard but I kept at it until I'd done the full thirty. I stood up and looked around. I was dismayed to see I was not the first one done. But I was far from the last one done, either.

I made eye contact with Daniel. I don't know why, but I nodded at him. He nodded back. All of a sudden, I felt like I wasn't quite so alone.

When the last bedraggled potential player dragged themselves to their feet, the coach blasted on the whistle again.

"Everybody, two laps around the pitch!"

"Is he insane?" someone blurted.

I joined the pack, working my way toward the front. I pushed myself hard, but I couldn't break into the ten fastest runners.

These guys are all elite. If I'm going to keep up, I've got to want it more than they do.

When I made it around the first lap, my legs felt like lead. Every breath I dragged into my lungs took a huge effort. If my heart could talk, it would have asked me why I wanted it to explode.

But I ran on. Which was saying something, as about a dozen or so guys had gassed out already. Some of them had fallen into fast walks, while others bent over with their hands on their knees. One guy staggered off the pitch and puked his guts out by the bleachers.

Boy, when I was halfway through the second lap around the pitch, I thought I was a goner. Sweat rolled down my forehead and into my eyes, stinging them so much I could barely see. I could have sworn the air was made of bricks because it sure was hard to breathe.

My legs felt like water as I staggered the last ten feet across the finish line. I didn't want to collapse like some of the other guys, so I carefully sat down cross-legged on the grass. I saw Coach staring at me hard. I guessed he was mad at me for taking it easy.

Coach blew the whistle, and looked at those of us who had made it across the finish line. Maybe half of those who had started remained.

"You guys take five," he said. "Bobby and Stan will dispense Gatorade."

Coach turned to those still straggling across the finish line.

"The rest of you can leave. I'm sorry. Better luck next year."

Most of those who failed slumped off the field without another word. But one boy tromped up to Coach and pointed a finger at his chest.

"You can't cut me! Do you know who I am? My dad and my grandpa played on this team."

"I know," Coach replied. "I coached your dad. Unlike you, he had some hustle. Better luck next year, kid."

"You haven't seen the last of me," the kid sputtered.

"Yeah, I just said, better luck next year."

Coach turned his back on the kid, and I felt hugely better. Coach Johnson didn't care one bit about legacies. He only cared if you could cut the mustard.

"Those of you who remain," Coach shouted, "probably think you're lucky. You're not. The ones who left, they're the lucky ones because we're just getting started."

He blasted on his whistle.

"Everybody on your feet! We're going to do some drills."

"But I just sat down," someone complained. I looked over to see a barrel-chested kid with thick, curly hair. With his short legs and stocky build, I wouldn't have thought he could run all that well. But he had been one of us who had made it.

"Aww, then go ahead, you can skip the drills," Coach said nicely.

"Really?" the kid asked.

"Yeah, you can skip the drills and walk your butt right off of my pitch. Or you can stop whining and show me what you've got."

The kid glared but he fell in with the rest of us as we were split into three groups. My group got paired with Coach, while the other two fell in with Bobby and Stan, the assistant coaches.

Coach led us to an area of the pitch with colored cones set up in pairs about five feet apart. I recognized the setup from Henry Raab's soccer practices. This was a Gate Game drill.

We were split in half, attackers and defenders. Basically, the attackers tried to get the ball through the cones, or "gates", while the defenders tried to harass and hinder them.

I wound up a defender on the initial go-around. And boy, was it a humbling experience. The first kid I went against juked me easy and got through all six gates in record time.

I did a little better the second time around, but it took everything I had. On the last gate, I overextended myself on a tackle and flopped onto the grass.

When we switched over and I got my turn as an attacker, I did a little better. Not great, but good enough to make up for my poor performance as a defender. I hoped.

Coach didn't say anything. He just stood off to the side, making notes on his clipboard. I wondered if he was still mad at me for sitting down after the laps.

CHAPTER 8

No Pain, no Train

"Remember, today is the tomorrow you worried about yesterday."

— Dale Carnegie

Our groups rotated, so we wound up with assistant Coach Bobby. Our next drill was pretty straightforward, a passing rotation game. I did really well on that one. I found that I could get in sync with the other player a lot faster than most of the other guys trying out.

When assistant Coach Bobby made notes on his clipboard, I noticed him smiling. I hoped that was a good sign.

We switched again, and our group faced assistant coach Stan. He had lined up six soccer goals in narrow lanes, about thirty feet apart from each other. I wasn't familiar with this drill. It seemed like everyone else knew what to do.

Embarrassed, I asked Coach Stan to explain it to me.

"This is a ladder drill, son," Stan replied with a smile. He had long blonde hair, and I had a good feeling women thought he was good looking. "You play one-on-one until someone gets three goals, and then the winners rotate and face each other."

"What happens to the losers?"

Stan shrugged.

"They're out."

I felt a chill run down my spine. Did he mean they were out of the drill, or did he mean they were out of the tryouts?

Fear mounted inside of me as I faced off against my opponent. Not only was he the boy who had come in first during the race, but I rarely spent any time as a goaltender, or a defensive player for that matter.

I would have to be aggressive and attack, attack, attack if I wanted to avoid being cut.

Me and the other kid crouched, waiting for the signal to begin. Stan went through the three lanes and placed a ball in the middle of each of them. My opponent was a little bit taller than I was, but I think we probably weighed the same.

He would have speed and a longer leg reach. I could pivot and change direction quicker and in a shorter space, though. We were pretty evenly matched, I thought.

Stan blew his whistle, and we both charged the ball. We both went for the tackle. I remembered what Johnson had told me back in the park and kept my body over the ball as much as possible.

My opponent managed to get the ball, but he kicked it out of bounds. That gave me a dribble in, per the rules of the drill. I juked his attempted tackle and kicked the ball cleanly into his goal.

We reset and started again. I managed to score on him a second time. But then he got back-to-back goals against me.

I was sweating and puffing when I finally got past his defenses and scored the third and final goal. Stan blew his whistle, and the lanky kid suddenly grinned at me.

"You're pretty good, Mr. Snoogie."

He offered his fist. After a second of hesitation, I bumped it.

"Thanks. So are you. I almost didn't beat you."

"I know. My name's Alex. You and me, we're going to tear it up as teammates."

"If we make the tryout," I said.

"Oh, we'll make it."

I made it through two more rounds of the drill before Coach Johnson blew his whistle and called time.

"Everybody take a hydration break. If you need to potty, now is the time," Coach Rex bellowed. He huddled up with his assistant coaches in the bleachers.

"Man, I'd love to hear what they're saying right now," Alex said.

"What are they talking about?" I asked.

"Oh, they're discussing who to cut and who to keep for the next round. They'll whittle us down until only the elite remain."

I really, really, really wanted to be one of those elite. It was sheer torture waiting for the coach and his assistants to decide who was going on and who was going to the showers.

We fell silent, all of us, as the coaches stood up and descended from the bleachers. I swallowed the lump in my throat. This was it. My future was about to be decided.

Coach Johnson walked to the center of the pitch, staring at his clipboard.

"If I call your name, I want you to line up over here."

He indicated the white border line. Then he started calling names. One by one, a dozen boys got up and joined the line. Many of them high-fived each other, and acted cocky.

My heart sank when Coach flipped the page on his clipboard and tucked it under his arm. He was done calling names. I was not chosen. I would not be on the team, not this year...

Coach Johnson turned to those who were lined up, the chosen ones.

"I'm sorry," he said, not unkindly. "But better luck next year."

I almost fainted with relief. Coach had switched things up and called the names of those he intended to cut. Was he trying to give us all heart attacks?

Then again, Alex, Daniel and the curly haired boy were all not chosen. I should have guessed the better players weren't the ones lining up.

"Those of you who are left, congratulations. You've made it to the final assessment. If you pass this next test, you're on the team. But this time, it's not about individual performance."

His eyes narrowed as he stared us down.

"This time, you will stand and rise, or fall and fail, as a team."

He glanced over at Stan.

"Coach Stan?"

Stan stepped up, staring at his own clipboard.

"If I call your name, come stand up here," he said, gesturing beside himself. "Daniel Haggin. Rob Dickenson. Bruce Halford. Andrew Brautigum."

His eyes turned right on me.

"Max Goalman."

I stood up and joined the others who had been called, wondering what was going on. We'd already made it to the finals, so why were we five being separated?

"The five students standing up here had the highest scores during tryouts today."

I was stunned to hear that, as much as I felt like I struggled.

"You'll notice two of them are Frosh. Congratulations, Daniel and Max. You five are the team captains. I want each of you to select three students to be your teammates."

We went down the line and chose our teammates. I picked Alex first and then the curly-haired, stocky boy. Despite his complaints, he'd done really well on the drills.

For the final pick, I selected the guy who'd smoked me on the first drill. I was surprised he hadn't been one of the team captains.

"Nice to meet you guys," I said as our teams gathered and the coaches set up the pitch for whatever they had in store for us. "I already know Alex. I'm Max. What are your names?"

"Han," said the kid who'd beaten me when I played defender during the drill.

"Like Han Solo?" Alex asked.

"No," Han said with a glare. "Like Hanzo. My family is from Japan."

"Nice to meet you, Hanzo," I said quickly, before either of them could get angry with each other. I turned to the curly-haired kid with the barrel chest. "And what's your name?"

He puffed his chest out even further.

"I am Percival Lucius Pringle III."

"Nice to meet you, Percy," I said.

"Percival," he said firmly. "I refuse to answer to Percy. I'm no peasant."

Alex rolled his eyes.

"Oh great. You sure you want this guy on our team, Max?"

"His defense is fantastic, even if his personality is not so much."

Percy...I mean, Percival glared at us, but he didn't say anything. I guess he was used to being called a jerk.

I looked out over the pitch and noticed the coaches had sectioned off the field with cones. They had split it into five different parts. Since there were no goals, I wondered what we were going to do in those sections.

I soon found out. Assistant coach Bobby blew his whistle and bellowed at us.

"Listen up because I don't like to repeat myself. We're

going to play some four-on-four possession squares."

"What?" I asked. Han and Percival seemed similarly perplexed. "I've never heard of this drill."

"It's something they only do in the professional leagues," Alex said with more than a little bit of pride. "Coach Johnson likes to use it because he says it builds great fundamentals."

"How does it work?" I asked. "I don't see any goals. How do you know who wins?"

"In possession squares, it's all about keeping control of the ball," Alex said. "Every time your team manages three successful passes, you score a point. Otherwise, it has all the rules of a normal game."

"But without the goals, which way do you move the ball? There's no up or downfield."

Alex shrugged.

"You move the ball toward whoever on your team is open. Trust me, it kind of takes care of itself."

I was starting to feel like Alex should have been our captain. Instead of getting jealous, I asked him to explain more. He obviously had experience.

He talked, and we listened.

"We don't have a full-sized field to play with, so it's going to be easy to get the ball out of bounds. We want to avoid that, because we'll have to throw in and possibly lose possession. Keep your passes short, too. We'll have to work together and try to create openings for each other."

Coach blasted his whistle. We faced off against the other team.

Daniel's team. I couldn't help but notice he'd picked the

biggest, strongest players available. But that could work against him in a passing game. Those big boys could wind up getting in each other's way.

We raced for the ball, Daniel and I in the lead for our teams. I swiped it to my left just before his foot made contact. Percival took the ball and dribbled it away from Daniel's teammates.

I ran along beside the pack. I wanted to position myself to receive a pass. Not from Percival, though. From Han, who was in a much better position to receive from Percy.

Percival shot the ball over to Han, who passed it to me. I was so excited I could have exploded. Three passes, we'd scored a point.

Daniel came up for the tackle. I only had a split second to react, and I did the same move I'd used in the park on reflex. Daniel was ready, though, and stole the ball with his left foot.

I smothered him as best I could, trying to prevent any hope of a pass, but he shot it over to a teammate. I almost collapsed in relief when Alex got possession of the ball, ending their passing chain at two and preventing a point.

I'd played a lot of games of soccer, some of them pretty grueling. But I'd never gone through anything like those tryouts. Coach Johnson pushed us so hard, and the culmination was this possession squares game that kept us just running, running, running.

In a conventional soccer game, there are lulls. When there's a throw-in or dribble-in, before a kickoff, and so on. In possession squares, we never stopped moving.

I sighed in relief when the coach blew his whistle. Then he had to go and open his mouth.

"All right, rotate teams!"

Most of us groaned. Now we had to play yet another game of possession squares. By the time we reached the final game in our mini round-robin tournament, everyone moved a lot slower than they had at the start.

In the last game, I was so exhausted I couldn't even keep track of the score. When we broke for water, I could have died.

While we all sat or laid around on the pitch, gasping like fish out of water, Coach Johnson blew his whistle. I cringed, but he motioned for us to stay down.

"At ease, boys. Tryouts are over."

A chorus of relief rang up from all of us. Coach Johnson laughed.

"You all did good today. You should be proud. But only twenty of you are going to make junior varsity. Tonight, at 7:00 PM, I'm going to post the names of our team roster."

"On, like, Instagram?" Percival asked.

Coach sneered at him.

"No, not like Instagram. I mean I'm going to post it on the bulletin board outside my office."

His eyes narrowed to slits.

"Now, listen up, and listen up good. If your name is not on the list, you are not on the team. Period. End of story. I don't care if you call your mommy. I don't care if you call your daddy. I don't care if you call the Dean, the Academy Chair, or the Secretary-General of the United Nations. You. Are. Not. On. The. Team."

His expression changed to something less stony.

"Now, if your name is on the list, report to this field at

4:00 PM Monday afternoon, sharp, for our first practice. And come ready to work."

Coach Johnson turned and left us there, sweating and panting on the pitch. It would be hours and hours before I found out if I made the team.

I would go insane, if I didn't explode first.

CHAPTER 9

Soccer to Me, Soccer to You

"I've never lost a game. I just ran out of time."

— Michael Jordan

The sun sat directly overhead when I got back to the dorms. Even though tryouts had seemed to take an eternity, it was only a little after noon.

Noon! I had six hours to go before I found out if I made the team. Talk about torture.

Exhausted as I was, I knew I couldn't sleep. I grabbed a quick shower and then flopped down on my bed, not caring that my hair was still wet.

I'm not sure how long I lay there. I kept playing the tryouts over and over again in my brain. I ran it back and forth like a video on YouTube, trying to figure out what went right, and what went wrong.

I felt like there had been more wrong than right. Nigel

woke up sometime around then and shuffled into the bathroom after a mumbled greeting.

When he returned, Nigel seemed a lot more awake. He looked at me and snorted.

"You look like you're about to explode. I take it you don't know if you're going to be on the team yet?"

I shook my head.

"No, not yet."

Nigel sat down in front of his computer and swirled the mouse around until the screen turned on.

"You think you made it?" he asked without turning around.

"I don't know. I mean, when the tryouts were about half over, I was in the top five."

He spun around in his chair.

"For real? Then you should be on the team."

"Yeah, but that was only the halfway point. Then we engaged in this torture called possession squares, and I'm not so sure I was in the top five after that."

He grunted and spun back around in his chair.

"So when do you find out?"

"Tonight, after the coaches post it on the bulletin board."

"Dang. Better read a book or something."

That made me think of something.

"Hey, is there a comic book store near campus?"

"Huh? How would I know that? I'm not a nerd."

I peered over his shoulder and snorted.

"You're playing an MMO fantasy game. That makes you a bigger nerd than me by far."

He laughed as his character appeared on the screen.

"You might be right, Mr. Snoogie. You might be right."

I groaned.

"I was hoping that wouldn't get around."

"Ah, it could be worse. Heard you stuck it to that Ramirez chick who saddled you with the name, though. Good job."

"I did get her with a pretty good zinger."

He looked over at me. I think he was worried.

"What's wrong?" I asked.

"Listen, don't make an enemy out of her. She's connected."

"Again, with the connections. I don't want to make her my enemy. I don't want any enemies, but..."

Nigel leaned back in his chair and stifled a yawn.

"But what?"

"There's this guy who was at tryouts. Daniel Haggin. I used to play against him back home. I don't think he likes me very much."

"So? That's his problem, not yours."

I wasn't sure I could agree with Nigel's outlook on life.

"Well, if we both make the team, it could be a problem. You need to be able to rely on each other out on the pitch."

"Out on the what? I thought pitching was baseball?"

I chuckled.

"The pitch is what we call the soccer field. Of course, we also sometimes call it the field."

"Sounds complicated," he said. I could tell Nigel was getting into his game more than listening to me, so I left him alone.

I tried to pass the time in a lot of ways. Watching soccer games just made me think more about the tryouts. I tried to nap but that didn't take, either.

Then it hit me: I was starving. I went to the cafeteria and loaded up on food. I felt like I could eat not just a horse, but the entire Kentucky Derby.

I think I had made it through two burritos and a full plate of Spanish rice when my phone buzzed. When I dug it out, I saw that Mom was calling.

On a video call.

I shuddered at the prospect of talking to my mother, much less a video call, in the middle of the cafeteria. After the Mr. Snoogie situation and my dad being, well, my dad, I already had enough problems with my popularity.

I had to let it buzz because if I'd declined the call, she would have known I was awake. I had to pretend I was at tryouts or crashed out asleep after.

But then I felt guilty for putting her off. I found myself a quiet spot in the green space between the cafeteria and the gymnasium and called my mom.

She answered on the first ring.

"Max, are you all right?"

That's how she answered. Not hello, not hi sweetie. She just assumed I was in trouble.

"I'm fine, Mom. How are you?"

"If you're fine, why didn't you answer me? You remember our agreement, right? You have to call me every Saturday."

"Yeah, but it's only like two, Mom. I was gonna call."

"You'd better. How's school?"

I sat up straighter, my heart thumping in my chest.

"Mom, you won't believe this place. Coach Johnson has us doing drills that you only see in international pro leagues. Guys were dropping like flies at the tryouts. I thought for sure I was a goner at least ten or twelve times."

"Good grief, Maxwell, that sounds horrible. Maybe you should come home."

My jaw fell open so hard, I heard it crack.

"Mom, no! It's not that bad. I mean, the tryouts were tough, but nobody died."

That I knew of.

"Well, you be careful just the same. I've heard those boys at Caldwell Academy play very rough."

"Not really, Mom. Besides, if you get too rough you get a card. Nobody wants to get red-carded out of a game, because then you're down a man for the rest of the game."

She sighed.

"At least it's not football. Real football, I mean, with pads and helmets. I still worry, Max, but I know how important this is to you. How did the tryouts go?"

"Um, I'm not sure."

I told her the whole story. When I wound it up, she sounded a lot more upbeat than I felt.

"Max, it sounds to me like you're a shoo-in. You were one of the team captains they picked, after all."

"Yeah, but there were so many good players, Mom. I'm not the only one who Coach Johnson scouted out, either. Daniel Haggin is here."

"Is that the boy who blew up our mailbox with fireworks two years ago?"

"Yeah."

She harrumphed.

"Well, you stay away from him. He's a bad influence. I need to go, I have a tutoring session coming up. But make sure you stick to our schedule."

"Yes, Ma'am."

"I love you."

I looked around to make absolutely sure no one could hear me but Mom.

"I love you too," I whispered.

"What?"

"I love you too," I said a little louder.

"What?"

"I love you too, Mom!" I down right screamed.

"I heard you the first time," she said with a giggle. "I just wanted to hear it again."

I ended the call, grumbling, and stood up. And you know who I saw, not ten feet away, filming me with her phone?

Augusta Lorena Sanchez Villa-Lobos Ramirez.

"Well, well, well, Mama's boy. What is it going to take for me to delete this video instead of posting it on the internet?"

I stood there, stunned, unable to speak. Why did I have such bad luck with this weirdo? Or was she stalking me or something?

"Will you give me all of your desserts for a month?" she asked with a cocky smile.

I knew that it wouldn't end with just my desserts. She would lord this over me for the next four years at Caldwell Academy. I would never be free of her.

There was another way, though. It was a risky move but just like in Soccer, fortune favors the bold. At least, that's what Pele said in an interview, once.

"Ah," I said, turning my back on her and waving it off. "Do what you want with it, I don't care."

I started walking away from her, then. Lobo stood there for a second, then followed me.

"I mean it. I'll put it on the net, and everyone will see."

"I said, I don't care."

"People will troll you on all of your accounts."

"My parents won't let me have social media, so I'll never see it anyway. Like I said, do what you want."

She stopped following me. I played it cool until I made it around the corner of the gym. Then I leaned against the wall and wiped the sweat off my brow.

When I peeked around the corner, she was gone. I hoped my little gambit worked. I had enough problems being Mr. Snoogie.

By the time I got back to the dorm, it was nearly five o'clock. I couldn't stand it any longer. I showed up outside of Johnson's office early. And I was not the only one.

"Greetings and salutations," Percival said with a slight bow of his head.

"Hi, Percival." I gestured at the other hopefuls who had gathered, about ten of them. "Looks like we're not the only ones who got anxious."

"Indeed. I'm pleased you selected me for your team, Max. It certainly helped my cause."

"Ah, no problem, Percival. I mean, you have some of the best footwork I've ever seen, and um, well, your, ah..."

"I'm built like a fireplug. That's what my Dad says, but he also taught me how to use it. I can smother a striker or midfielder and they'll never get a clean shot off at our goal."

I smiled, admiring his confidence. He talked like we'd already made the team.

I wished I could be that sure of myself. It felt like I'd drunk a gallon of acid, my stomach was so messed up. I just kept thinking how awful it would be if I didn't make the team. Not just having to leave Caldwell, but facing my parents and my friends and telling them all that Max Goalman was a failure.

The clock moved so slow, I swear it had stopped altogether. As time ticked toward six o'clock, more and more potential players arrived. Alex joined our little gaggle, as did Han. It sort of felt like it had with Roberto and Jimmy — the same, but different.

"If we make the team, what position do you want?" Alex asked when it was about ten til six.

"Oh, that's easy," Han said. "Midfielder. I can play

offense and defense equally well, and I can run all day."

"And you're modest," Alex said with a snicker. "How about you, Percy?"

"It's Percival, you cretin. And obviously I would be a wingback. Let me swing the pendulum your way, Alexander. What position do you want?"

"I'm pretty flexible. I think I can play offense a little better than defense, though. What about you, Max?"

"Attacking Midfielder," I said without hesitation. "Just like Messi."

Alex nodded, as did Percival.

"I can see that. You've got the right skillset to be an attacking midfielder."

I spotted movement at Johnson's frosted glass office door. It got real quiet in that hallway, real fast.

Johnson appeared. His gaze flashed over the whole group of us without really focusing on anyone in particular. He held a piece of white paper in his hand.

No one spoke as he tacked it onto the bulletin board. Heck, I don't think anyone even breathed. I know I didn't.

I expected a mad rush for the board, but instead the opposite happened. No one wanted to be the first one to go and look and see their fate.

"Oh, this is ludicrous," Percival said, huffing over to the paper. "I must know..."

He stopped moving, stiff as a board.

"Percival?" I said.

No answer.

"Percy?" Alex asked.

Percival turned around, wearing a huge smile.

"I told you, it's Percival. Now, if you'll excuse me, I need to inform my father that I made the team."

"You made the team! That's great, Percival," I said.

After that, the potentials all lined up to read the paper. Some guys slumped their shoulders and shuffled away in defeat. Some hooped and hollered and danced like they were on fire.

I inched toward the paper, dreading and hoping what I would see. The names were arranged in alphabetical order. I looked for the letter G, and...

Goalman, Maxwell.

A giddy heat formed in my chest. I think I went yahoo or something. I don't remember. The next thing I knew, I was running back to the dorms, feeling like I'd just won a zillion dollars in the lottery.

Don't get me wrong. I knew there was a lot of hard work ahead. But I'd made the team.

When I got back to the dorm, I tried calling my parents, but they didn't answer. I figured that since it was a Saturday, they were probably having a date night. They would call me when they got out of the movie or whatever.

Nigel woke up...again...and took one look at my face before declaring that I'd made the team.

"You know what this means, right?" He asked.

"Um, I'm going to be put through more brutal drills than ever?"

"No, we have to celebrate. I have a friend who stole

some beer out of the bursar's office. You wanna come and drink it with us?"

I shook my head.

"No thanks. I have to watch what I put in my body, but I'm not judging."

I'd practiced saying that in the mirror because my dad told me to. It would allow me to avoid giving in to peer pressure while making it clear I was not, in my dad's words, a 'snitch.'

"It's cool," Nigel said, which relieved me. I was afraid he was going to pressure me about it. "Hey, if you don't want beer, there's probably going to be s'mores. You do eat those, right?"

"I love s'mores," I said reluctantly. "I guess I could go for a little bit, we have to make it back by eight for curfew."

"Aw, they never check to see if we're actually in our rooms. They just lock the doors after eight."

"Lock the doors?" I gasped. "How will we get back in without getting in trouble?"

"We sneak in by climbing up the downspout on the south side of the dorms. I do it all the time."

I shook my head.

"No, if I get caught outside after curfew, I could get kicked off the team. If I get kicked off the team, I get kicked out of school."

He tilted his head to the side.

"Really, my dude?"

"Yeah, really. Athletic scholarship. I'm one of the poor kids, remember?"

He nodded as if that made perfect sense.

"All right. Well, how about if you come down to the bonfire, eat one s'more, and then you can go back to the room?"

I sighed. It seemed like it would be easier to indulge him than it would be to say no.

"Okay, fine. But just one s'more, and then I'm leaving."

"Of course, just one S'more."

I should have gone with my gut because it was a long walk to the bonfire. When we got there, I didn't see any s'mores. Just a bunch of burn-outs listening to loud music and acting like they were super cool grown-ups.

I barely made it back to the dorms in time for curfew. My parents called back and congratulated me on making the team. That felt pretty good, even if I knew they'd interrupted their date night just to call me.

Pretty soon, I realized how tired I was. I climbed into the bed in my clothes and passed out in seconds. When I woke up, it was Sunday afternoon. I guess I was pretty tired.

When Monday morning came around, I got to worrying again. I feared the classes would be super hard. I also didn't like having to wear a collared shirt and tie just to sit in a classroom.

To tell you the truth, the classes were harder. Things moved a little bit faster than back home, and the teachers assigned us more homework than I was used to. It wasn't anything I couldn't handle, though. That came as a relief.

It was still kind of hard sitting through my last class of the day, and not just because it was my worst subject, math. I kept thinking how in just one hour I would have my first official soccer practice at Caldwell Academy. I was so excited I had a hard time concentrating.

At last, the clock struck three, and classes ended for the day. I practically ran to the dorms so I could change. They hadn't issued us uniforms yet, so I put on my old one from Henry Raab.

I stuffed my Valhallas into my duffel bag along with a bottle of water and a low-carb, low sugar snack and jogged over to the stadium. I just hoped Coach Johnson had gotten over my sitting down during the tryouts.

CHAPTER 10

It's a Tryout, Not a Cryout

"My favorite machine at the gym is the vending machine."

— Caroline Rhea

First team practice with the Caldwell Cannons.

I was so nervous on the way to the stadium I almost threw up. Between the brutal tryouts and the difficult academics, Caldwell Academy had me reeling. Getting into the familiar routine of soccer practice would get my head on straight.

Or so I thought, until I arrived at practice.

I barely stepped through the archway onto the field when Coach Bobby locked his angry gaze on me.

"Goalman! Get your butt in gear and start weaving!"

I froze because there was a ton of activity on the field. I had no idea what group I was being instructed to join. I understood some of the drills, like Dibble, Sprint, Dribble.

That one was easy, and involved dribbling the ball to the center pitch line and then running your butt off back to the other side.

Other drills looked sort of like one-on-one games, with players sectioned off by cones into long rectangles.

"Goalman, what's your problem? Are you a spectator or a sportsman?" Coach Bobby bellowed, his face turning bright red. "Get over there and start weaving!"

At least the second time, he pointed to where I was supposed to go. I spotted a line of boys, each of them taking a turn dribbling the ball through a slalom of cones. Duh, weaving. I should have known.

I ran over there instantly, but that didn't stop Coach Bobby from blasting on his whistle and yelling at me to move it, move it, move it. It looked like I'd made another coach mad, and all because I didn't know what kind of drill he meant.

I joined the line of players, finding myself behind Percival.

"Salutations, Maxwell," he said.

"Hey, what's up, Percival?" I looked around the field. "I thought practice started at nine?"

"Officially, but everyone who's anyone knows you have to show up early."

"I did show up early..."

Percival snorted.

"Not early enough, apparently."

I swear, I could feel Coach Bobby's eyes boring into me when I stepped up for my turn. Dribbling is something I've done almost since I could walk. It should have been no trouble to weave in and out of the cones.

But when I took my turn, nerves took over. As one of the top players at tryouts, everybody who wasn't in the middle of their own drill watched me. All of those eyeballs focused on little old me created a whole new type of pressure.

I choked. I'll be the first one to admit it. I totally choked on that drill. I moved the ball all of three feet before I knocked it out of bounds. Coach Bobby blasted his whistle like a train engine.

"Get that ball back in bounds, pronto!"

I tried — I really did — but the next thing I knew, one of the cones flopped over and I nearly tripped. When I finished the drill, a lot of guys laughed at me, including Coach Bobby.

"Did you wake up with two left feet this morning, Goalman?"

I slumped my shoulders and endured the ribbing. Daniel took his turn on the weaving drill. I know it's not good to wish ill on other people, but I really was hoping he'd blow the drill just like I did.

Instead, he dribbled through those cones like a champ. It made me feel even worse. Especially after it was over and Coach Bobby praised him.

"Now that's more like it, Daniel! Keep up the good work."

Daniel shrugged.

"It's just a simple weaving drill, no big."

The smirk Daniel sent my way let me know he knew exactly what he was doing. It really rankled, and I kept thinking of how great it would be if a bird did a number on Daniel's head right about then.

"Don't let him get to you, Goalman," Han said, slapping

me on the shoulder. "It was only a drill. What really counts is on game day."

Han helped me feel a little better, but my problems continued for the entire practice. There were so many drills I'd never performed before. I didn't bomb as badly as I had on the weaving, but it sure seemed like I struggled more than I should have.

The drills just kept coming. They lined us up into five groups, like for a relay race. Only the coaches didn't give us batons. They arranged tires in a grid pattern, then distributed different colored sashes. I was on team green.

"What's going on?" I asked Percival.

"It's a tic-tac-toe sprint. It builds endurance, and teaches you to change direction quickly."

I looked back at the gridwork of tires and recognized a basic tic-tac-toe grid. Then I did the math.

"Wait, are we competing against the red team?"

"Yes," Percival said. "When you run out, you can either put out a jersey or move one of the other team's jerseys. The first team to get three in a row wins."

Coach Johnson blew his whistle. The kids at the front of the lines took off like crazy. I shouted encouragement at our team. Our guy got out there first and put down a jersey in the middle, the best spot. The other team, though, moved it off the spot instead of placing their own.

I figured out the drill pretty quickly, and it was gonna be brutal. Basically, we would be at a stalemate, until guys started to gas out. Then it would come down to who had the best endurance.

Which just figured that I was on a team with three fullbacks, who probably have the worst cardio of any other position.

We gave it our all. I booked up and down the grass three separate times. The first time, I put a green sash next to another one on the outside edge of the grid. But the other team blocked our three in a row.

My next time up, I started to feel the strain in my legs. I moved the enemy's jersey off the grid before they could score.

But my last trip, my legs felt like water and I just wasn't as fast as normal. I couldn't do anything but watch while the other team plopped down a jersey and scored the third in a row, winning the game.

"It was only a drill, Max," Percival said, clapping me on the back.

"I know."

It still hurt to lose, though. Especially when I knew that the Coaches were watching closely. Doing well on the drills would increase my chances of getting on the starting lineup.

I did a lot better at the circle passing game. We split up into groups of ten, and practiced passes to each other. I was pretty proud of the fact that our group never once let the ball go out of bounds, or missed a pass at all.

At one point, midway through practice, I was so hot I stuck my head under the water fountain. I gasped like a fish as the cold water filtered through the sweat to reach my scalp.

"Are you okay, man?"

I looked up into the face of Alex. I was past pretending it was okay.

"This is hard," I gasped. "This is the hardest practice I've ever had. Why does it seem like everyone else already knows what to do on these drills?"

Alex tilted his head to the side.

"Didn't your personal coach have you do these kinds of drills?"

"Personal coach?"

Alex's eyes widened.

"Oh, right, I heard from your roommate you were, um... yeah. Don't stress about it, Goalman. You killed it in tryouts. Besides, the whole point of practice is to get better, right?"

"Yeah, you're right."

I did feel a teensy bit better, especially when we stopped the drills and played a mock half-game. Playing felt a lot more natural than practicing.

Somehow, Daniel and I wound up on opposing sides, just like in the park back home. He managed to sneak past our defenses and score the game's only goal. My side tried to even things up, but we ran out of time.

When practice finally ended, the team staggered off the field and into the locker room. I wasn't the only one totally exhausted. Only Han seemed to still have energy left, though even he was diminished from his usual self.

"Man, the coaches were all over us today," Alex groaned as he laced up his street shoes. "I'm going to start dreading practice if this keeps up."

A lot of guys spoke up right then, with some choice cuss words thrown in for good measure. Razzing on the coaches was a time-honored soccer tradition, so I didn't think anything of it.

I even added my two cents.

"That Coach Bobby has the most evil eyes I've ever seen," I said. "I'm pretty sure he sleeps in a coffin."

I was expecting my joke to get some laughs. Only Percival chuckled, and he stopped all of a sudden, staring right at me. Or so I thought.

"Maybe we should all wear garlic necklaces," I said, still trying to get someone to laugh. Everyone just looked more and more nervous and scared, though. "You know, in case he tries to get us to join the legions of the undead."

"I'm Italian, Goalman. I love garlic."

I stiffened up at the sound of the voice right behind me. I didn't have to turn around to know it was coach Bobby... but I did anyway. He stood there, hands on hips, glaring at me so hard I thought I would die on the spot.

The rest of the team made a hasty retreat, but I remained, held captive by his gaze. If he really was a vampire, I'd be a dead man. I flinched when the door slammed behind the last kid.

Coach Bobby continued to glare at me.

"I'm sorry," I said in a tiny voice.

"I'm not worried about your insults, Goalman. I've heard better insults from more creative people. What I AM worried about is your cruddy performance on the field today. I expect more out of someone who Rex Rocket hand-picked for this team."

I hung my head in shame. He snorted and then left me alone. I sank onto the wooden bench beside my locker. I felt like crying, but the tears just wouldn't come.

How had this gone wrong so quickly? I thought getting through tryouts would be the hard part. But now it looked like things were only going to get harder.

Back home, I was the best player in my neighborhood, the best player on my school team. I guess I'd gotten used to that status. How would my dad say it? Oh yeah. I was a big fish in a little pond.

Now, though, I swam in a much bigger pond with much bigger fish. I could have claimed to be the best back home. Here, that wasn't the case. I had been one of the top five players in tryouts.

But at the first practice, I knew I was near the bottom. Alex mentioned having a personal coach like he was talking about the sky being blue. Like everyone had a personal coach, just a statement of fact.

Even though I wasn't really poor, at Caldwell, people were starting to look at me as one of the financially unfortunate. I'd thought my Valhallan cleats were a big deal, but lots of other guys on the team had them, too. A few even had the really, really expensive Valhallans that I would never dream of asking my parents to buy for me.

I had another practice scheduled on Friday afternoon. Instead of looking forward to it, I dreaded it. I sure felt homesick after the first practice. So much so that I called my folks.

CHAPTER 11
The Phone Ranger

"I am only human, although I regret it."

— Mark Twain

Mom picked up on the first ring.

"Max, how are you? Are you eating right? Are you sleeping okay? Is anyone being mean to you?"

"Hi, Mom," I said. "I'm fine, I guess. I mean, I'm eating and sleeping okay. Nobody's really being mean, except maybe Coach Bobby. I don't think he likes me."

"What makes you think that? Do I need to call the school?"

Panic shot through me like a lighting bolt. Everybody knows you can't have your parents call the school! I had enough problems with being Mr. Snoogie as it was.

"No! No, please don't do that, Mom."

"Well, if he's giving you problems, I think I should be involved."

"He's not giving me problems, not exactly, um...he's just a hard coach. I can deal with him."

"Are you sure?"

"Yes, I'm sure."

"Well..."

Her voice made it seem like she didn't really want to believe me.

"All right, Maxwell. But if you change your mind, Mama Bear will come running to protect her cub."

"Thanks, Mom," I said, covering my face with shame. Thank goodness I hadn't put the call on speaker. Mama Bear! My parents are out to destroy my social life, I swear.

I talked to Mom for a while, and then she went and got Dad out of the garage so I could talk to him, too. It felt good to hear my parents' voices. I guess all those times I thought they were annoying weren't as bad as I'd remembered.

Then they put me on the phone with my little sister, Emma. She'd been spending the last month of summer vacation with our grandma because Nana had felt lonely since Gramps passed on. Fortunately for me, unlike most little sisters, Emma isn't a brat.

"Have you met any girls, Max?" she asked me.

"Yuck, no way! I've been focusing on school and soccer."

"Well, Mom is worried that you're going to get a broken heart."

I had to laugh at that.

"Ha! You tell Mom that my heart beats only for soccer."

"All right, but you have to do an extra good job at Caldwell."

"Why is that? I mean, yeah, that's what I want to do anyway, but why do you care?'

She sighed as if I was the dumbest person ever.

"I'm going to go to Caldwell someday! If you ruin our family reputation before I get there, I'll never forgive you."

"You could always change your name."

She blew out a razz.

"Bye, bro. Don't be a doofus."

"You're a big enough doofus for our entire family."

Then all of a sudden, my chest really hurt. Not physically, I don't guess. Just like a pressure was there, and I really missed my sister and parents bad.

"I love you, Emma. Mom and Dad, too. I won't ruin our rep, I swear."

"I know how you feel, Max," she said.

"You do?"

"Yeah. I love ME too."

Then you know what she did? She ended the call just like that. For some reason, I wasn't mad. I laughed, and that tight feeling went away in my chest, at least a little bit.

Next practice, I showed up early — real, real early. I was one of the first people there. In fact, the Upperclassman Varsity soccer team wasn't done with their practice yet. One thing I could tell for sure: the coaches weren't any easier on the older students. In fact, they may have been even harder on them.

I kept my eyeballs glued to the field, soaking up everything I could. I even got my Language Arts folder out and took notes. A shadow fell over my page while I was trying to sketch out the passing pattern the older kids used.

Annoyed, I looked up to see a tall, lean boy with shaggy brown hair.

"Hey, do you mind stepping to the side?" I asked. "I'm trying to write."

"I can see that."

He sat down next to me and reached a hand toward the notebook. Then he looked at me like he wanted me to do something. I finally realized what he wanted. Reluctantly, I handed over my notes.

The kid stared at the page, his eyes barely open. He flipped through the half dozen pages I'd already finished, then handed the notebook back.

"You must really be into soccer to take six pages of notes. What's your name, kid?"

I found it kind of funny that he called me kid when he was maybe two years older, tops.

"Max Goalman."

His eyes widened.

"Mr. Snoogie!"

Oh, I wanted to punch him for that! But he made up for it pretty quick.

"I heard you've got mad skills, Mr. Snoogie."

I looked him up and down, trying to figure out what his deal was.

"Are you a coach?" I asked at last. He seemed way too young, but if he were a player, he should have been on the practice field. I didn't see any obvious injuries to prevent it.

"No, not at all. I'm a player. Technically."

His face wrinkled up. I could tell something really bothered him.

"What do you mean, technically?"

"I'm officially on the team, but I'm sitting this season out."

"How come?"

His eyes changed like he was looking at something really far away.

"I tore my ACL in a game last season. I did my last round of surgery over summer break, but the doctors won't let me back on the field yet."

It felt like someone stabbed me in the gut.

"That's terrible!"

"Yeah, tell me about it. I'm hoping by winter break, they'll let me play again. Until then, I'm still required to come to practice, but I got nothing to do."

"I'm sorry, um...what was your name?"

"Paul. Paul van Dijak."

He shook my hand, and then we both looked at the field.

"How are you liking Caldwell so far?"

"It's um, it's pretty intense," I said. "It's a lot different than playing soccer for my old school. I never even heard of some of these skill drills before."

"Coach Johnson uses the same drills they do in FILA, on the professional level. You couldn't ask for better training, Max."

"Yeah, I get that. I kind of think one, maybe two of the coaches don't like me, though."

"Which ones?"

"Coach Bobby and maybe Coach Johnson," I replied.

"Hmm." He stared out over at Johnson. "I don't know about Johnson. He's hard to read. But if Coach Bobby is all over you, that's a good thing."

"It is?"

"Yeah. He always comes down harder on people he thinks have the highest potential."

I didn't know if I could believe what Paul said or not, but it did make me feel a little better.

"I hope you're right. I kind of messed up some of my drills last practice."

Paul slapped me on the shoulder.

"Keep working hard, and you'll do fine. You remind me of myself, Mr. Snoogie."

"Why?" I blurted.

He grinned.

"You're the only other player I've ever seen who takes notes while watching another team practice. I'll see you around, Goalman. Your team's about to take the field for practice."

He was right. I ran to the locker room and changed before returning to the pitch. The coaches didn't start us on drills right away, though. First, Coach Johnson stood in front of us and stared us all down for about a full minute before he spoke.

"Those of you who are standing here on this field today are on the team...but that doesn't mean you're going to be starters."

We all looked at each other nervously. No one wants to be benched, especially on a permanent basis.

"To be a starter, you have to have three things."

Coach Johnson held up one finger.

"Number one, you've got to have gas in the tank. If your cardio isn't up to snuff, you're not going to start. Period, end of story."

I felt a little more comfortable. I have cardio all day long!

"Number two," Johnson said, holding up a second finger. "You have to have the skill and the polish. I don't want dribblers. I want GREAT dribblers. Get it?"

A lot of us nodded, and I got all nervous again. I felt kind of dumb, thinking I would come to Caldwell and just dominate everyone else. Little fish, big pond. I would really have to work hard to be as good or better than some of the other guys on the team.

"Number three," Johnson said, his eyes getting real narrow like a snake. "And this is the most important of them all. You have to be HUNGRY. You have to want to be on this pitch, playing soccer, more than anything else in the entire world."

He looked around at us and sneered.

"Well? Are you hungry?"

"Yes," I said, along with about a half dozen other people. Coach Johnson cocked an eyebrow at us.

"I can't hear you. I said, are you hungry?"

"YES!" A lot more folks joined in.

"I still can't hear you. Are. You. HUNGRY?"

Everyone screamed so loud my ears hurt afterward.

"Good!" Johnson bellowed. "Now let's attack these drills! I want everyone in top shape for the All-Prep Futbol Tournament."

I felt confused. I'd never heard of this tournament before, but then again, I usually followed pro soccer, not junior soccer.

There was no time to ask. The coaches divvied us up between them. I got put with Coach Stan, much to my relief. He still worked me hard, but he didn't seem to have it in for me like Bobby did.

When we were on a water break, I asked Percival about the upcoming tourney.

"All-Prep is a huge deal, Maxwell," he said, using that tone of voice he has where he tries to sound all smart and stuff. "It's an international tournament. We'll be competing against prep academies from all over the world. If you win, you get the Eagle."

"The Eagle?"

He snorted at my lack of knowledge.

"You really don't know anything, do you? The Eagle is a seven-foot-tall trophy. Coach Johnson cleared a space for it several years ago in the trophy case...but he's never won it."

"Never?" I gasped. "I thought Caldwell had a fantastic soccer program."

"We do," he said, puffing his chest out. "But so do a lot of other schools. If we're going to win, we have to be the best, of the best, of the best."

The best of the best of the best? Man, talk about pressure! If I was a chunk of coal, I'd have been a diamond after hearing that.

I worked extra hard that afternoon, busting my you know what like nobody's business. Only, I wasn't the only one. Everyone upped their game and had extra spring in their step.

I think I did pretty good at practice. None of the coaches seemed upset with me, at least. But they straight up praised Daniel, at least twice that I could see. If he was getting praise and not me, that meant he had a better chance of making the team.

It would be so embarrassing to lose a starting position to one of the guys I used to play in the neighborhood. I didn't hate Daniel, but I really wanted to outdo him. Like, really, really bad.

We were all a pathetic, sweaty mess after that practice, but we were fired up as all heck. I went to bed that night dreaming of winning the Eagle trophy for Coach Johnson.

But first, I had to git gud! I had to improve my skills and make the starting lineup.

"Git gud," I mumbled to myself as I went back to sleep. "Git gud."

CHAPTER 12
Having a Ball

"I'd run over my own mother to win the Super Bowl."

"To win, I'd run over Joe's mom too."

— Joe Jacoby and Matt Millen

Pressure, pressure, pressure!
Sometimes, I felt like I was going to explode leading up to the tournament!

And I'm not just talking about soccer pressure, either, though that was the worst of it. The schoolwork got more intense, too.

Like in my Communications class, I never even heard of one of those before, but the main thrust was writing and giving speeches. It would have been fine if I could have picked my own subject. I would have given a speech about soccer.

But the teacher randomly assigned us our speeches. I wound up having to give a speech on the Taft-Hawley Act. I never heard of that, either.

You want to know the worst part? We weren't allowed to use the internet to do our research. I had to go to the library and dig through a bunch of books until I found the information I needed. My roommate, however, had a simple solution.

"Dude," he said, kind of laughing. "Why don't you just do what everyone else does and cheat?"

"Cheat?" I sputtered. "I can't cheat!"

"Why not?"

"Because it's not right!" I snapped back. "And what if I got caught?"

"Not right?" Nigel frowned. I knew then that he didn't think there was anything wrong with cheating. "If you say so. Do it the hard way if you want."

"My Mom and Dad say the hard way is usually the best way, if you want to learn and grow."

Nigel started laughing.

"Who in the heck wants to do that? It sounds boring."

I guess I could have had a worse roommate. At least he didn't snore.

Between all of my classes and soccer practice, I had no time for anything else. A funny thing happened around the two-month mark of my first year at Caldwell: People started disappearing from my classes.

At first, it was only a couple of empty desks, but then it got more noticeable. I finally asked Percival after practice one day. He seemed to always know what was going on.

"They're dropping out, of course," he said with a snort.

"Dropping out? Why?"

Percival put a hand on my shoulder and looked me dead in the eyes, almost like my parents did sometimes.

"Max, you must simply understand that not everyone is an elite like you and I."

"An elite? I'm not elite, though. I'm one of the poor kids."

He shook his head.

"Not what I meant at all. Some students simply cannot handle the pressure of Caldwell Academy. Those poor unfortunates are forced to drop out. It's sad, really."

Dropping out. I hadn't even considered that as an option. That night, I lay in my bunk and stared at the ceiling, thinking about what Percival had said.

At first, I was like, no way would I ever drop out. No way! It meant too much to me. I couldn't be the next Messi if I didn't have the training and polishing that Caldwell could give me.

But the more I thought about it, the more the idea kind of stuck in my head. If I went back home, I could sleep in my own bed, with no Nigels in sight. I could see Mom and Dad and Emma every day and see all of my friends, Roberto, Jimmy, Dallas, Houston, all of them.

I even thought that I could still make it as a pro soccer player, even without Caldwell. It got even harder not to think about dropping out when the tournament got closer, and the practices grew more and more intense.

We'd been practicing and fake-competing against each other for so long, people started being able to read each other. Daniel especially, got the ability to read me. Whenever we faced off in drills or practice games, he had my number. Every time.

Daniel either plowed me over or out-dribbled me. It got

so frustrating I wanted to cry. One day, he collided with me and made my nose bleed. It was a legal hit, but it still hurt. I think Coach Johnson knew I needed a break and told me to go to the infirmary even though my nose stopped bleeding real fast.

The doctors told me my nose wasn't broken, and they told me to ice it. The pain in my nose didn't bother me, really. I'd been hurt worse in soccer games.

What really hurt was that Daniel and a couple other guys on the team really started to outshine me. It made me want to join the unfortunate dropouts, real, real, real bad.

I was holding my phone in my hands, trying to work up the courage to call home again, when a knock came at my door. I got up to answer it and was surprised to find Paul.

"Get your gear, Max."

"What? Why?"

He grinned.

"Just get your gear and meet me on the pitch."

Paul walked down the hall and vanished around the corner. I almost wondered if I didn't imagine him being there. But I put on my gear anyway and went to the pitch.

Paul waited for me, his shadow stretched way, way out by the setting sun. He didn't look like he'd been sick over the summer. He looked like a darn champion, all lean muscle and poise. Paul had one foot on a soccer ball as I approached.

"What are we going to do?" I asked.

"We're going to make it so you don't get pwned on the pitch by that Daniel jerk," Paul said with a laugh. "I'm going to coach you."

"Why?" I blurted.

He cocked his eyebrow at me.

"Because even though you're really good, you haven't had the benefit of private tutoring like a lot of guys have. I'm just trying to help you get better."

"No, that's not what I mean," I said quickly. "I mean, why are you helping me?"

His face got this real weird look on it. He didn't look at me when he answered. He looked at the setting sun instead.

"Sometimes, you have to think about what kind of legacy you leave behind."

"What?"

He shook his head.

"Never mind. Look, Max, they won't let me play this semester. So I'm living vicariously through you, all right?"

"What does vicariously mean?" I had to look that word up before I could write it in this journal.

"It means, I'm going to help you be great, so I feel better about not being able to play myself. Now, if you go look in the trophy case, you'll see my name on a lot of them. I can help you a lot, Max, but if you don't want me to..."

"No!" I shouted. "No, I definitely want the help! I need it!"

Paul laughed.

"Okay, settle down. Man, you really are a soccer maniac. Just like me. From now on, you and me are gonna have our own practice sessions. Six a.m. and six p.m., except on days you have regular practice or a game."

"Six a.m.?" I blurted. I was not excited about getting up that early.

"I didn't stutter," he replied. "You want this or not, Max?"

"I want it! I so want it!"

"All right, then. Six and six."

"When do we start?" I asked.

He grinned.

"Right now."

He started slowly dribbling the ball toward the distant goal.

"What do I have to do?" I asked.

"Take the ball away from me."

I launched myself after him, jogging up behind. I tried to steal the ball, but his footwork was incredible. He crossed and uncrossed his legs, he used every side of his foot to keep the ball moving, and he continuously faked me out.

I didn't even get my cleats to touch the ball, let alone steal it. At last, he called for a break, and I bent over, hands on knees, huffing and puffing like I was gonna die.

"What was that you did?" I asked. "Just now."

"A double lunge," he replied. "It's a great fake-out trick. Here, let me show you how it's done."

I struggled to learn that move, but after about an hour, I could do it halfway decent. Paul declared that was enough for the day but reminded me that I needed to be there at six a.m. the next day.

Boy, was it hard to wake up that early! My body just wanted to go back to sleep. But the thought of getting the better of Daniel and making the starting lineup got me moving. When I arrived at the pitch, the sun wasn't even up yet. It was just a red line on the horizon.

Paul looked fresh as a daisy, as if he'd had all the sleep in the world. He didn't say hi or anything. He just started dribbling for the goal.

That's the way our practice sessions went. For the first half, we played one-on-one. He usually got the better of me, but he also taught me new tricks every time. I finally realized what he was doing. He was showing me a technique and then teaching me how to do it after.

Then, one day, Paul pulled something that floored me. I was coming up on Paul, about to tackle and take possession of the ball. I was super excited because I knew I had him. I just knew it!

But then, Paul switched up his stance, and the ball just vanished. I looked around like a crazy man, trying to find it. The next thing I knew, Paul was dribbling the ball all the way to the goal. Where had he hidden it?

"Did you swallow the ball?" I asked, frustrated and hot and tired.

"No. You have to follow the Rainbow, Max."

"The rainbow?"

He grinned, then dribbled back a little bit away from me. Paul picked up the ball with both his feet and jumped in the air. He kind of threw the ball softly behind him.

Then, his trailing foot caught the ball on the heel, and he sent it into a beautiful arc over his head. It landed in front of him, and he started dribbling again. The whole thing was so smooth, so perfect, and so awesome, I wanted to cry.

"What was that?"

"That's the Rainbow. Also called the Rainbow Flick. Because the ball comes down like a rainbow, get it?"

"I do get it. Teach me, please!"

Tyrone's bushy brow raised in the air.

"I can teach you, Max. It's hard, one of the hardest things to pick up in soccer. But I know you can master it."

He started by having me keep the ball constantly bouncing in the air, reflecting off my cleats. It's a lot harder than it seems! I kept losing the ball. I'd seen guys in the big leagues do tricks like that, but I'd never learned to do them myself.

Paul pushed me to do well, but he never came across as bad as the coaches, especially Bobby. I hate to say it, but it kind of felt like Paul was the big brother I never had.

Between the early morning practices with Paul, the regularly scheduled soccer practices with the team, and my own research watching the upperclassmen play, I spent about twenty hours a week on the soccer field.

At the end of my first week of this hectic schedule, I collapsed into my bunk. I didn't play video games, I didn't write in this journal. I did nothing but sleep. Oh, sweet sleep! I never knew how much it meant to me until I got to Caldwell Academy.

In fact, I slept so hard I didn't wake up until Saturday morning. Mom's ring tone — the exact same one I'd used for Darth Vader, if you catch my drift — played and woke me out of my Rip Van Winkle act.

"Hello?" I said or tried to. It's hard to talk when your tongue is dried and stuck to the roof of your mouth. I reached for my sports drink bottle, but it was empty.

"Max? Hello? Are you all right?"

I went into the bathroom and ran the tap, cupping water into my hand so I could splash it into my mouth. Mom just kept right on going, like a rhino.

"Max, can you hear me? What's wrong with your voice? Oh no, have you been kidnapped?"

"No, Mom," I rasped. My tongue was loose, but my super dry throat made me sound like a cheesy super-villain.

"Who are you? What have you done with my baby boy? If you hurt him, I'll shove my rolling pin so far up your — "

"Mom!" I sputtered, able to speak at last. "It's me, Mom. I haven't been kidnapped. Nobody would bother kidnapping me at this school. My friend Percival would get a lot bigger ransom."

"Max, what's going on? Are you sick? Don't tell me you slept with the window open?"

I sighed and rubbed my eyes.

"No, Mom, just a dry throat. I slept for a long time, and I was really thirsty."

I told her about my busy week. Mom liked the idea that I'd made a friend in Paul, but she didn't like my extra practices.

"Max, do you remember when I was trying to get my master's degree and teaching full-time?"

"Yeah, Mom. You were always napping. At the dinner table, in the movie theater, at Cousin Henrietta's wedding — "

"Never mind that! In fact, never bring up your cousin's wedding again, or I'll ground you for life. Anyway, do you know why I was always napping, sweetie?"

"Um, because you were tired?"

"Yes, you're right. You see, Max, it takes more than just eight hours of sleep for you to feel rested. You need to rest your mind as well. It's great that you're getting all this soccer practice in, but I want you to take some time for yourself."

"Mom, soccer practice is taking time for myself. You know how much I love it."

"Not what I mean, honey. Your father told me I was burning my candle at both ends. Do you understand what that means?"

"I think so, Mom. Like, you're going to end up with no candle at all."

"Exactly. It's okay to play video games, or read comics, or even just sit on a hillside and look at the clouds."

"The clouds? I'm trying to be a soccer player, Mom, not the new channel five weatherman."

"Just try it sometime. Trust me, it will do you a world of good."

I agreed to go and look at the clouds sometime. It sounded weird to me, but it was important to Mom.

CHAPTER 13

Humble Pie for Breakfast

"NA rich man is nothing but a poor man with money."

— W. C. Fields

The morning practice with Paul continued. I wanted to work on mastering the Rainbow, but Tyrone kept putting me through the same basic drills over and over again. He tried to make me tackle the ball away from him, but that was easier said than done.

Not only did Paul have longer legs than I did, being two years older, he also had endurance for weeks and weeks. It was like trying to keep up with a bolt of lightning that could turn on a dime and give you some change back.

When Paul wasn't humiliating me on the pitch, Coach Bobby was right there to take up the slack. I don't know what I ever did to him to make him hate my guts. I was pretty sure that he did, though.

After our midweek afternoon team practice, I sat on the bench in the locker room trying to recover the energy to walk back to my dorm room. The practice had not gone well for me.

I felt like the other players were all improving way faster than me. They were off and running, while I lagged behind.

When I finally got up the gumption to walk back home, I trudged past the Coaching Office. The frosted glass door was shut, but I could see three shapes inside.

"So, let's talk about the strongest players," Coach Johnson said in his gruff voice. He always sounded a little bit mad even when he wasn't.

I knew I shouldn't eavesdrop, but I wanted to know what the coaches thought of me so bad. I stayed rooted to the spot, trying to be quiet as a mouse. I barely even breathed.

"Daniel, no question," Coach Bobby said. It kind of annoyed me to hear him say that. I had to admit Daniel was pretty good, though. "Great footwork, he can play offense or defense, and I don't think that kid ever gets tired."

"Agreed," Coach Stan said in his higher-pitched voice. I could just make out his shape through the frosted glass. "But as good as he is, he's not a very good team player. He tries to hog the ball, he refuses to pass when it would be the best move strategically...I'm not sure if he's coachable on this."

"It's our job to make him coachable," Coach Johnson said in a growly voice. "Who else?"

"I like Percival. Not a highlight reel player, but his defense is nearly impenetrable."

It made me happy to hear that Percival had impressed them. It also made me a little bit jealous. I strained my ears when they talked again.

"Agreed," Coach Bobby said. "Kind of an attitude problem, but he doesn't show it on the field. He's as good a team player as they come."

Coach Johnson grunted.

"I wish I could say that Max Goalman was on my top three list," Coach Johnson said. "I thought that kid was something else when I saw him in the wild. Now, I'm not so sure I made the right decision."

My heart sank, and I wanted to just crawl into a hole and die. That's not the kind of thing I wanted to hear from my coaches.

"I've been telling you all along that Goalman is gonna peak and fade fast," Coach Bobby said.

I covered my face with my hand. How much worse could it get?

"You remember," Coach Bobby went on to say, "right, Rex? You remember when he was being lazy and sat down during practice."

My worst fears had come true. I knew that Coach Johnson had been giving me the stink eye that day.

"Lazy? You're wrong, Bob." Coach Johnson snorted. "I was looking at Goalman that day and thinking, *that's a smart kid, using the opportunity to rest and regain energy.* If I'd have thought he was being lazy, I'd have busted his chops then and there."

Hope flared in my chest, and the weight of the world didn't seem so bad. So, I had a chance! They hadn't given up on me yet.

"I agree with Coach Johnson," Coach Stan chimed in. "I mean, don't forget that Max hasn't been playing on an elite team for his entire life, like most of our roster. Plus, I get the feeling he's a Pikachu."

"A what?" Coach Johnson said.

I remembered the Pikachu from those really old cartoons. I didn't understand what it had to do with me or soccer.

"A Pikachu," Stan said again. "Look, in the world of trading card games, you can pick a monster that has really high statistics starting off, or you can start with one that has lower statistics, like Pikachu."

"What a geek," Coach Johnson said with a sigh.

"No, hear me out. I have a point, I swear. So, Max is like that. He has lower statistics right now, but his growth potential is much higher. The monsters with high starting stats peak early. Max has nowhere to go but up. Besides, it's not like he's among the bottom three players."

I didn't stick around to hear who they didn't like. I ran out of there, and all of a sudden, the world didn't seem so rough.

Weird, I didn't feel as tired, either. Don't get me wrong, I still collapsed into my bunk and slept like the dead every night. I just didn't feel as down about everything.

My performance at team practice improved little by little. But I still couldn't compete with Paul. He had insisted he would not tutor me on mastering the Rainbow until I could tackle the ball away from him.

The tournament was getting closer and closer, and I wanted to be able to use the Rainbow so bad I could taste it. I started seeing Paul and that soccer ball in my dreams at night. I sketched in the border of my notebook, trying to come up with new fake outs and dribbles and switch-ups to throw him off.

Paul sure didn't make it any easier on me, either. He constantly taunted me whenever I failed a tackle, or he took possession, or I stumbled and fell on my face during a drill.

"Come on, Goalman!" he shouted one afternoon, eyes narrowed to slits as I seethed in the grass. "How are you going to win the All-Prep Tournament if you can't even take the ball away from me?"

I dragged myself to my feet and tore after him. This time, I was going to make him eat those words.

"Oh, now you're getting angry!"

Paul's grin took on a sinister edge. His eyes got all hard and glinty, too. I knew he wouldn't make things easy on me. He dribbled the ball upfield toward the pair of duct-taped cones we'd fished out of the dumpster last week. If he made it through the cones, it would be considered a "goal."

He'd already scored seven times on me, while I hadn't gotten him even once.

"You think you can use that anger?"

Paul spun around and ran backward. I caught up quickly because no way would he run near as fast backward. But when I went to tackle, his feet moved in a blur. I couldn't keep track of the ball, and he tucked it neatly under his cleated heel.

"You want this?"

A frustrated growl tore out of me. I went after him like I was possessed by an evil spirit. If pure rage could have gotten me the ball, boy, I'd have had it. But it seemed like the harder I tried, the more easily he kept away from me.

I threw everything into a low sweep tackle. He kicked the ball with his heel into a short arc, then jumped over my leg and landed on the other side facing forward. I flopped and skidded across the grass, getting some in my eyes and nose.

Between sneezes and through a curtain of tears, I saw him pass between the cones. I wiped my face with my forearm and then grabbed handfuls of the grass. I think I roared like a dinosaur.

Paul dribbled the ball back to me. I didn't even look up at him as he stopped.

"What happened?" he asked.

"I lost."

He snorted.

"Yeah, but why?"

I looked up at him, gritting my teeth in frustration.

"Why? Why? Because you're so much better than me."

"Why? What makes me better?"

I stood up fast and got up in his face.

"How can you even say that? You're older than me, taller, you have longer legs, and you're just so dang fast!"

Paul laughed, shaking his head and flicking the ball onto the top of his foot.

"Oh man, you really think that's why you failed? You regularly beat that Daniel kid from your old neighborhood, right?"

"So?"

"So?" Paul shook his head, his smile fading. "So, Daniel is older than you, taller than you, has longer legs, and he's probably a little faster than you."

"Gee, thanks for the pep talk."

"I'm not finished, Max. He's all of those things. He has

all of those advantages on you...but you used to beat him all the time. Why is that?"

Paul didn't seem to be making fun of me. I knew he wanted me to really think about it. So that's what I did. I replayed all of the games I played against the jerks from Jericho Junior High in my brain.

"Well," I began, "Daniel tends to get too focused on one thing, you know? Like, he should be worried about our fullback coming up to tackle the ball away from him, but instead, he's only thinking about lining up his shot for a goal."

"Right. What else?"

"Um...he gets all angry and worries about his grudges more than the game. I used to do things just to make him angry, so he'd play bad."

Paul grinned.

"Now, are you getting it? Being angry doesn't help you play any better. When I was injured, I used to get really angry, but the doctors told me that doesn't help you get healthy. In fact, it can hinder you."

I shook my head.

"I'm confused. Are you saying I should be without emotions like those pointy eared guys from Star-Trek?"

Paul laughed so hard he cried.

"Oh, good grief," he said, wiping his eyes. "No, of course not. You need to feel the game if you want to win the game. But feeling it, wanting it, craving it...that's not the same as being angry. Anger is a waste of energy. Anger at me or anger at yourself because you think you're not good enough."

I wiped the sweat out of my eyes and sighed.

"I'm not really angry with you, but I guess I am mad at myself."

"Well, stop it."

He slapped me with his damp sweat towel. I yelped and retreated a safe distance.

"No more being mad at yourself, Max. And don't forget, this is supposed to be fun. Play because you want to because you enjoy it, not because you'll be mad at yourself if you fail."

Play because I wanted to? It seemed stupid and obvious, but the more I thought about what Paul said, the more it bounced around in my brain.

"Now, if you're up to it, let's play one more round. If you score on me, I'll buy you a snow cone."

"Unicorn?"

"Whatevs."

"All right. Threetwoonego!"

I tackled the ball away from him and dribbled like nobody's business down the pitch. He came running up behind me, catching up fast.

I sidled toward the edge of the pitch, getting perilously close to out of bounds. He used my position against me, trying to make me nudge out or make a mistake and give up the ball.

It could have made me mad. I tried not to get angry, though. Instead, I thought about how bad I wanted to score the goal and how I'd seen Messi getting edged out by Manchester in just such a manner a couple of years back.

What had Messi done? Something I had yet to master. I

had to try, though. I'd been practicing late at night in the green space behind our dorm. I hoped I could pull it off.

Just when my cleats were an inch from going over the line, I put on the brakes and switched up my footwork. Paul expected me to do just that.

But I had something else up my shin guard. As he moved in to take possession of the ball, his foot held almost like a sweeping hook; I made my move. Kicking the ball behind me, I caught it with my trailing foot and heel-bumped it straight up into the air.

Fully committed, Paul slid right out of bounds, his foot whiffing through air where the ball had been a split second before. The black-and-white sphere came down in a perfect arc, bouncing in front of me as I took off toward the cones and victory.

"You son of a gun!" Paul shouted after me. "You've been practicing the Rainbow!"

Yes, I had. I dribbled the ball through his cones, slowing down to savor the moment. Paul came jogging up, shaking his head and laughing.

"You see, Max? You understand now that anger is not your friend?"

I shook my head.

"No, anger's not my friend. You are."

I stuck my hand out, and after a second, he shook it.

"You're ready for the tourney, Max."

CHAPTER 14
Just for Kicks

"The rules of soccer are very simple: if it moves, kick it. If it doesn't move, kick it until it does."

— Phil Woosnam

The All-Prep Academy Soccer Tournament.

It was all I could think about. Or at least, all I wanted to think about. I still had classes and homework and stuff. I still had to call my parents once a week and assure them I wasn't about to crack under the pressure.

But if I had my way, I would have been thinking about soccer all the time. Coach Johnson likes to say, "Eat, sleep, play soccer, and repeat." That was starting to be my motto, too.

My soccer practices leading up to the tournament grew more and more intense. Most of the time we didn't do drills, we did mock games. It soon became clear that Daniel and I were both up for the coveted spot of attacking midfielder.

I didn't just want the position because Messi played it. I really did think I was the best fit. Daniel was good and could have been the midfielder and done okay. But I really thought he should have been a Striker. That way, he could take advantage of his freaky laser focus and work only on scoring.

The extra practices and coaching with Paul helped. He expanded my game in more than just physical ways, too. As the time for the tournament drew near, we started to spend more time on strategy and tactics.

"I'm not going to lie, Max," Paul said as we hunkered over his tablet. "This tournament is gonna be brutal. The teams are all elite, and they want it bad. Some of them aren't afraid to cheat to win, either."

"But the refs call them out on it, right?"

"Yeah, when they see it. And assuming the refs haven't been paid off. It's just a rumor, understand, but I've seen some pretty bad calls in my day. Just something to watch out for."

As if I wasn't freaked out enough! Sometimes, I thought Paul's sense of humor could use some work. Seriously, he needed to take his act on the road...and leave it there.

The last week of school before the tourney dragged on forever — or it felt like it, anyway. Coach Johnson canceled practice, saying he wanted us well-rested before the tournament. I still worked with Paul in the mornings and the afternoons, but I still had more free time than before.

So you know what I did? I slept. A lot. Not only that, but since the tournament was taking us away from Caldwell Academy I had to do extra homework and exams that I would be missing the following week. Otherwise, I would have fallen behind, and I couldn't afford that. I had to keep my grades up in order to stay on the team.

At last, Friday morning arrived. I didn't have to go to my classes because we were all meeting at the stadium parking lot. I packed up my overnight bag and my Valhallan cleats and made it there half an hour early.

A thick fog hung over the parking lot. I could see the headlights of the buses, looking spooky in the fog. As I got closer, I spotted the Coaches, and several of my teammates, all lined up and waiting for the go-ahead to board the buses.

I walked up to find Percival and Alex chatting, both of them looking tired but happy. They turned their smiles on me as I joined them.

"Here he is, Max Goalman," Percival said. "Are you sufficiently prepared for the monumental task ahead of us? I dare say it's Herculean."

"Herculean? I've never even looked at another...never mind," I said, shaking my head. Percival could be hard to understand at times. "I hope we're all prepared. I heard from Paul that this tournament is pretty rough. Like some of the guys even cheat and get away with it."

Alex shrugged.

"People who cheat only do it because they aren't good enough to win fair and square. The Caldwell Cannons don't need to cheat. We're going to win this tourney."

"Yeah, right we are!"

We fist-bumped, but I didn't really feel as confident as I sounded. I wondered if Alex really thought we were going to win or was just saying that.

"Hey, how come there are two buses?" I asked.

"The other bus is for the girls' team, the Lady Cannoneers. We have got to win so the girls don't show us up. I hear they're the number one pick to win it all in their division."

"If the girls can win, then so can we," I said, trying to sound like I really believed it.

Percival looked around, his face twisted up like he smelled something bad.

"What's wrong, Percival?" I asked.

"I'm looking for a place where I can rest my Italian leather backpack without sullying it. I want to look at my tablet."

"Why? Can't it wait until we get on the bus?" Alex asked.

"No, it cannot. I simply must see the tournament brackets. They were to be posted at nine a.m. this morning."

I checked the time.

"That was five minutes ago," I said.

"Exactly," Percival replied.

"So take out your tablet already," Alex grumbled.

"I told you, I must find a place where I will not sully my — "

"Fancy Italian leather backpack, yada, yada, yada," I said. "What if I got your tablet for you? Then your backpack could remain safe and unsullied on your shoulders."

Percival sniffed.

"I suppose that would be agreeable. Just don't root around in there. The tablet is in the pocket right at the top."

I unzipped his backpack.

"You know, this is a nice backpack," I said. "Oh, look, here's the tablet, but why is there a pair of women's underwear?"

"What?" Percival sputtered.

"I'm just kidding. Here."

I handed him the tablet. He gave me a dirty look before using his thumbprint to unlock the device. He quickly navigated to the official tournament website and then zoomed in on the screen on the brackets.

"This is a single elimination tournament, Max," Percival said, holding the screen so all three of us could see it. "If we lose, we are out. Simple as that."

"Then we can't lose," I said. "Who are we facing first?"

Percival zoomed in the screen a bit more so we could read the names more clearly.

"Exeter-Cross Prep Academy?" I said. "Never heard of them."

"They're like Caldwell, but because their stupid school is on the coast they think they're better than us," Alex said. "Their soccer program isn't that great, but their coaches make up for it with redshirting."

"Redshirting?" I asked.

"It refers to when a student is purposefully held back to repeat a year of school in order to keep them playing on the sports teams," Percival said.

"I still don't get it. They flunk kids on purpose?"

"Yeah, so they end up being older, stronger, and more experienced than the kids they'll be playing against."

I gasped.

"That's a cheat!"

"Yeah, exactly," Alex said. "If we can manage to get past E-Cross, then we'll either be facing La Forge Academy or Picard Prep. Both of them have top-notch programs."

"What happens if we make it past them?" I asked.

Percival smiled and jabbed his finger in the center of the bracket.

"That puts us in the finals against the winner of the Western bracket. If we win that...then we win the tournament."

"But we have to win," I said. "If we lose even once, we're out."

"That's the way a single-elimination tournament works," Alex replied.

More of our team showed up, and soon, the Coaches barked at us to line up and board the buses. I really wanted to talk to Coach Johnson, me, and everyone else. We really wanted to know the answer to one singular question.

Who would be the starters?

Making the team was one thing, but everyone wanted to be a starter. That meant the coaches thought you had what it took to help the team win. If you didn't start, it meant you weren't one of the elites. You were just a backup.

I really didn't want to be a backup. I imagine no one else did, either.

I wound up sitting next to Alex, which worked out well. Sometimes, Percival was hard to take. Alex and I chatted back and forth about the upcoming tournament. We didn't talk about who would be a starter, though. That was just too much nerves for either of us to take.

La Forge Academy was hosting the tournament this year. We had a six-hour bus ride ahead of us, split into two halves. Already, I was looking forward to the midpoint, when we would stop for lunch.

We stopped at a type of restaurant my dad always calls a "greasy spoon." I never understood why because the silverware wasn't greasy. He never explained. The whole team was so super excited. We talked as much as we ate. And we ate a lot!

Eventually, the coaches came down on us hard for being so noisy and disturbing the other diners. That put an end to our lunch. After we piled into the bus, I fell fast asleep, and I wasn't the only one.

I woke up to the sound of a lot of excited voices. Rubbing my eyes, I looked around, still half-asleep, to see my teammates pressing their faces to the bus windows and staring at something.

When I joined them, I laid eyes on the La Forge Stadium. The place was huge, with at least twice as much seating as the Cannons pitch. Probably why they picked this place for the tourney.

La Forge Academy sat on a slow-moving green river. We crossed an ancient-looking stone bridge to get to the campus itself. I peered over the edge at the water, the waves splashed white with bright sunlight.

"Is it just me," I said, "or is their campus a lot cooler than ours?"

"It's not just you," Han said, peering out the window beside me. "Oh man, is that a castle? They have a literal castle?"

The bus passed between two guard towers. One of the

towers had a big banner hanging off it. The banner looked like one of those old-timey paintings. A bunch of guys were kicking around a small round object in an open field.

I got the impression the La Forge Academy had been playing soccer for a very long time.

"Are you seeing what I'm seeing, Percival?"

Percival snorted.

"Yes, as long as what you are seeing is pretentiousness writ large. You'd think La Forge invented soccer."

Coach Johnson stood up at the front of the bus and blasted on his whistle until we all grew silent.

"Listen up, Cannons, and listen up good. From the moment you step off this bus, you're representing three things. Caldwell Academy, the Cannon Soccer program, and yours truly."

He jabbed a thumb at his own chest.

"So you had all better be on your best behavior. No spitwads. No pranks. No sneaking around after curfew. And absolutely no fights! Anyone who even gets near a fight is off the roster for the entire tournament. You understand me?"

"Yes, Coach," we all answered in a sing-song way.

"Good. You'll each be assigned a room for the weekend, and you'll have a chance to settle in. Then we'll gather in the main dining hall for supper, courtesy of our hosts, La Forge Academy."

"Dining hall? What is this place, Hogwarts?" Daniel said, which got a few laughs.

"Quiet," Coach Johnson snapped. "Don't load up on junk calories at dinner. Take reasonable, balanced proportions so you'll have the energy to run up and down that pitch and score some goals."

The bus lurched to a halt and we all started lining up to exit. I gripped my overnight bag so tight my knuckles popped. My first major tournament! I had butterflies the size of dinosaurs in my stomach.

They assigned us to our rooms, which we had to share with a teammate. I wound up rooming with Percival, which could have been worse. It could also have been better. His tendency to blast classical music got old pretty fast.

An elderly La Forge staffer came and knocked on our doors one by one to tell us to come to dinner. We didn't cause any problems on the way to the dining hall. Not just because of what Coach Johnson told us, but also because we were stunned by everything we saw.

I thought Caldwell Academy was super fancy when I first started going there. It didn't hold a candle to La Forge. On the way to the dining hall, we passed by statues of leaping centaurs, an ivy-covered living wall with little waterfalls coming off of it, and students practicing their horseback riding.

Sure, Caldwell had the horses, too, but they looked so much cooler in La Forge's sort-of castle.

A staffer bellowed at us to take the first open seats, so there was no choosing who I sat next to. The food they spread out for us was pretty good, but it was a little cold since we were the last team to be seated.

I didn't mind the food so much because my focus was on the other teams. This was my first time seeing them in person, and I wanted to size them up. The team from Exeter sat next to our table.

The Exeter team looked both relaxed and arrogant at the same time. It's like, they "knew" they were the best team but they were low-key about it. It made me want to beat them even more.

There wasn't much I could tell about them without seeing action on a soccer pitch. But I could tell a lot of the guys on their team looked a little old. Redshirting, Percival called it. Redshirting when they flunked kids on purpose to keep them in the soccer program another year.

Sitting next to Exeter was La Forge. I noticed their plates were a lot less full than the rest of ours.

I nudged Percival and pointed at the other table.

"Listen, maybe we should eat what the La Forge guys eat. Remember what Coach said about not loading up on junk calories."

Percival's brows climbed high on his face.

"Sage advice indeed, Maxwell. I'll pass the message along this way; you do so that way."

He pointed down the row of seated Cannons, and I nodded. I didn't understand what sage had to do with any of it, though.

We finished dinner, and then we had to listen to a bunch of speeches while we waited for dessert. Not only did the headmaster of La Forge have to go on a long-winded spiel about the honor and nobility of the tournament, but all the other team coaches got to talk, too.

Honestly, I had trouble staying awake at that point. The speeches were so super long and boring, and they had almost nothing to do with soccer.

I'd come to La Forge for one reason, and that was to play soccer. That's what I wanted to do, not listen to speeches and stuff.

At least the dessert wound up being worth the wait.

They called it a Soccer Sundae. A scoop of vanilla ice cream with chocolate panels made to look like a soccer ball made up the main dish. But then some genius in the kitchen decided to sandwich the ice cream ball between two chocolate chip cookies.

I didn't care if the La Forge team ate it or not. No way was I going to pass up on that dessert! It tasted better than it looked, and by the time I finished, all I wanted to do was sleep.

As tired as I was, I found it hard to actually get to sleep. Once we got back to our rooms, I wound up staring at the ceiling instead of snoozing. For a while, I thought Percival was sleeping soundly on the bunk beneath me. But then, he spoke.

"Maxwell? Are you awake?"

"No," I said with a groan. Tired as I was, I didn't want to talk to him or anybody.

"Of course you are. Another unfamiliar bed. Just when I'd gotten used to the peasant quarters at Caldwell, too."

"My dad always said if you can't sleep through anything, you're not really tired."

Percival chuckled below me.

"That's rather witty. I hope you don't mind if I steal that?"

"I don't mind, Percival. It's not mine, anyway."

He fell silent, and I hoped he was asleep. But then he went and ruined things by talking again.

"Maxwell, can I ask you a question?"

"You just did."

"Ah, you know what I mean. It's a given in the vernacular that I mean the question I'm about to ask."

I sighed and rolled over until I could thrust my head over the side of the bed.

"What is it, Percival?"

"I was just wondering if you were nervous about the tournament."

I wanted to say that I wasn't. But it didn't feel right to lie.

"I'm pretty nervous, Percival. We're playing Exeter first thing in the morning, and those guys are huge."

"Yes, indeed. And to be honest, they will present the least of our challenges in this tournament."

"The least?"

He nodded.

"You would have to be crazy not to be nervous, Maxwell. Just don't let your nerves get in the way. You're our secret weapon in this tournament."

"Secret weapon?"

He grinned.

"Just wait and see. And try not to despair if...things don't start on the best terms for you."

I groaned and pulled myself back onto the top bunk.

"I hate it when you get septic."

"Cryptic."

"Gesundheit," I snapped back. "Good night, Percival."

He finally did shut up after that. Thank goodness. I managed to catch some sleep, only to be awakened by a sharp knock at the door.

"Percival, Maxwell, get your butts up! Breakfast only comes once a day, and I want you two fueled up."

I went to the door, still half asleep, and opened it.

"There you are," Coach Johnson said. He looked somewhat spiffier than normal. At least he had on a new polo shirt and wore a shiny new whistle on a string around his neck. Plus, he was wearing pants. I hadn't seen him in anything but shorts since I started at Caldwell.

"Coach Johnson," I said, feeling like I should keep talking for some reason. "Um, we're really nervous."

"Good. Just let it fuel your play. Don't let nerves hinder you. Use them to be your very best."

I nodded, but I didn't really understand. How was I supposed to use the gnawing ache in my belly to my advantage?

It was one of those things adults said when they were in a hurry and not really paying attention. Coaches Johnson, Bobby, and Stan all moved down the hallway, rousing our team members one by one.

I went back inside the room and brushed my teeth before getting dressed. Percival just rinsed with mouthwash and stumbled along in his soccer gear.

"Don't you care if you get food on your soccer gear, Percival?"

He snorted and waved me off.

"Not at all. I will not sully my uniform like some — "

"Peasant?"

Percival glared at me.

"That is what you were going to say, isn't it?"

He snorted.

"Not necessarily."

Breakfast had plenty of options. I avoided the pancakes. All that sugar and empty calories wouldn't fuel me for long before the inevitable crash.

Instead, I loaded up on fresh fruits, lean ham, and raisin bran muffins. I barely tasted the food because all I could think about was our game.

After breakfast, we were given time to change before meeting up at the stadium. I raced down the tunnel, afraid I would be late. The dull roar I heard in the tunnel turned really loud when I stepped onto the pitch.

My jaw fell open. I couldn't believe how many people were in the stands. Just about everyone's parents had come to watch them.

Mom and Dad said they would try to attend, but I didn't hold out a lot of hope for that. I knew that they were busy, and taking four days off work is a lot for them.

But I kind of got my dad to agree to bring the whole family to the tournament finals...if the Cannons made it.

I guess that gave me a little more motivation to win and go all the way. But first, we had to make it past Exeter.

We all did a warm-up on our half of the pitch. Nothing too strenuous, just some light drills to loosen us up. More and more people filled the arena stands, and I even saw television cameras covering the match.

All of a sudden, I felt really small. This was for real, a real soccer arena, a real tournament. Did I really belong there?

I had to believe I did. Otherwise, I'd be disappointing way too many people.

Coach Bobby stepped up as we finished practice. He stared at the tablet in his hand and then lifted his gaze to take us all in.

"If I call your name, line up here."

He indicated the white line behind him. We all looked at each other, real anxious. We all knew that whoever got called to stand on that line would be a starter.

I hoped desperately that my name would be called. Percival made the starting lineup. So did Han and Alex. But after ten slots had been filled, I still stood amongst those not chosen.

Bobby stared at his tablet, then looked up at us. My heart quickened when he looked at me, but then his eyes kept right on going — until they settled on Daniel.

"Daniel. Join the lineup."

Daniel grinned ear to ear and jogged up to join the line.

"The rest of you hit the bench, but be ready to come in at a moment's notice," Coach Johnson said.

I felt sick to my stomach as I trudged back to the bench. I hadn't been chosen as a starter. I'd pinned all my hopes on being a starter, but instead, I was just a spare.

It felt like the death knell of doom when I sat down on the bench. I watched the others form up. Coach Johnson went with a 4-4-2 formation. Kind of a basic strategy, I thought, but I was kind of bitter at the time.

Our team struggled to retain possession of the ball. Daniel

was fast and strong and good, but he kept letting himself get isolated by the other team's defense. They smothered him to the point he couldn't get into a good scoring position. Most of the time, he couldn't even pass.

If not for Percival and Alex, who were in the fullback position, we probably would have Exeter score. I got really worried at one point when the Exeter striker lined himself up for a shot on our goaltender.

But Percival came in with a swift if somewhat clumsy-looking slide tackle. The ball smacked away to Alex, who passed it to Daniel. I sat back down on the bench, my heart no longer beating quite as fast.

I saw Coach Johnson, and tried to flag him down. He was too busy watching the game and bellowing out orders to notice me, though. I resolved myself to the fact I might not get to play in the game at all.

Doubt started to plague me. I wasn't sure if I was good enough anymore. Had I really come all the way to Exeter just to warm a bench with my butt?

At halftime, our coaches had a little powwow amongst themselves. They started making substitutions, and I got excited...

Only to find myself not chosen again. Most of the team had been replaced but for Percival and Daniel.

Even I could see that Daniel was getting tired. His legs no longer moved in a blur across the pitch, and sweat clung his shirt to his body.

Ten minutes into the second half, neither team had managed to score. Coach Johnson looked over at Coach Stan, and they nodded at each other.

"Goalman!" Stan bellowed. "You're in. Daniel, you're out."

I guess Daniel was pretty tired because he sure didn't argue as he jogged past me to take my place on the bench. I was in the best possible position for me now, attacking midfielder.

Coach Johnson set our formation to 4-3-3, meaning he wanted aggressive attempts to score a goal. On the throw-in, I took possession of the ball and dribbled it toward the enemy goal.

Now, I was in my element. My heart thundered in my chest. My cleats flew over the grassy pitch. My mind raced with a thousand thoughts at once. Look out for that tackle. The big kid wants to take possession, don't let him. Slow down and look for a pass; they're getting too close...

Swarmed by Exeter players, most of them a full head taller than me, I looked for a chance to pass. Our center was open. I used a fake out Paul taught me to juke the defending players and dove into a slide kick.

The ball spun like crazy as it shot across the grass. Our center got possession and dribbled toward the goal. I took off after then, as did the guys who had been about to cream me earlier.

The whole mob of us caught up as our center passed to the striker. I wondered what he was thinking because the Exeter guys were about to surround our striker.

Our striker pivoted on his rear leg and hooked the ball with his leading foot. He sent it bouncing perfectly in front of me. I realized that I had a clear field all the way to their goal.

Boy, I went after that ball like my life depended on it! The other team tried to keep up as I dribbled along the field, but I left them behind.

Then it hit me: I was way fresher than everyone else on the field. I milked the advantage to the fullest. While everyone else gassed out behind me, I pushed on toward the goal.

The goaltender's eyes focused on me like a jungle cat sizing up prey. He knew I was coming. That didn't mean I couldn't score on him. It did make it a lot harder, though.

I slowed down to line up my kick. The goaltender dropped into a slight crouch, ready to dive in any direction to stop the goal. Exeter's fullbacks charged in like elephants toward me. They were bigger than me, older. I admit, I was afraid.

I could have taken the shot. I didn't know if I would score, though. Swiveling my gaze around, I spotted our other midfielder. I didn't know the player well; I didn't even know his name yet. I did know he was like me, a replacement player.

If I took the shot and made it, I would prove myself to the coaches. Maybe enough that they would let me start next time. But my teammate was in a better scoring position, being closer to the goal and at an ideal angle.

It would mean giving the glory to someone else, but like Coach Johnson says, there's no I in team. I decided doing what was best for the team would be better than doing what was best for me.

I scrunched up my face and drew my leg back as if I were trying to kick the ball through the goaltender's chest. Everyone, the fullbacks and the goalkeeper, all reacted, shifting their movements to block me.

Which means they fell right into my trap.

Instead of murdering the ball with a full-on toe kick, I used the side of my foot to slap the ball laterally. It spun across the grass, sending up little wisps that caught the sunlight. My teammate caught the pass, perfectly in sync with me, and then just kind of batted the ball into the goal.

The blast of an air horn was only slightly louder than the roar of the crowd, not to mention the beating of my heart. I jumped up and down, so happy we'd scored a goal I couldn't stop freaking out. Me and the midfielder hugged each other as if we were old friends.

"What's your name?" I asked.

"Pietro. Thanks for giving me the pass."

"You were in a better position!"

We jogged back to our half of the pitch as the refs went crazy with their whistles. They were threatening us with an offsides penalty. I guessed they took the tournament pretty seriously.

"Great job, team," Coach Johnson yelled from the sidelines. "Especially you two! But don't get cocky..."

I couldn't hear the rest of what he said because the other team kicked off and the crowd roared with excitement. Running down the pitch, tracking the black-and-white ball in the air, listening to the cheers of the audience, it was all surreal.

For the first time, I felt like a real soccer player. Not just some kid who goofed off at his local park. For the first time, my dream of being the next Messi didn't seem so far away.

But I had to get through this game first. Coach told me not to get cocky...

I glanced over at Pietro.

"Let's get the ball and keep it!"

It was hard to talk while running full out, so I pointed at the game clock. Less than three minutes remained in the second half.

If we could keep the ball in our possession, the other team wouldn't have a chance to score. Maybe it wasn't the most valiant strategy, but then again, they were redshirting a bunch of giant kids against us.

The ball bounced down in front of Pietro. Alex jogged up behind him as Pietro dribbled, moving diagonally across the pitch.

I got into position, deeper back on our half of the field. Just when the Exeter giants were about to smother my teammates, Pietro passed to Alex, who then passed to me in the next heartbeat.

The Exeter guys weren't expecting us to move the ball toward our goal, so I had zero enemy players around me. I dribbled, moving diagonally, just like Pietro had. When things got hairy, with a lot of defenders trying to tackle the ball away, I passed to Alex, who then passed to Pietro.

Everything was going great. Until Pietro passed the ball back to me, and I turned around to see a big, knobby elbow in my face.

Whap!

I don't know quite what happened, other than I got hit in the face with a tall kid's elbow. I wound up sitting on the pitch, holding my bleeding nose as the Exeter guys desperately tried to move the ball down the field toward our goal.

"Ref!" Coach Stan screamed. "That was a blatant foul!"

"Contact was inadvertent," the ref said back.

I couldn't agree, but it didn't matter. I had to get up and get back in the game. I struggled to my feet and stared down the pitch. It was hard to focus my eyes after getting smashed in the nose.

When my vision cleared enough to see, it didn't look good. Most of the Exeter players were on our half of the pitch. They weren't even worried about defense anymore. They focused solely on overwhelming our defenses and scoring a goal.

I rushed toward the melee, my cleats sailing over the grass. My nose hurt, and it was hard to breathe, but I charged on ahead anyway.

The Exeter striker juked a tackle by our fullback and spun in a tight circle, keeping the ball bouncing off his feet. The guy was good, really good. I rushed in and knew my only chance was a risky sliding tackle.

Just as the striker wound up for the goal-scoring kick, I slid in and bumped the ball back toward their half of the pitch. The whole mob of us chased after the ball, but we all knew the truth. The air horn blasted, signaling the end of the second half.

I thrust my right arm in the air. My left arm was busy trying to stop the blood spilling out of my nose. Coach Stan came jogging up, his blue eyes full of concern.

"Are you all right, Max?"

"I think so. I think it's just a bloody nose."

Stan didn't look convinced of that. He cried out for a medic. A real nice lady with pretty dark hair sat me down on a bench and checked my nose out.

"I don't think it's broken," she said, her white gloves stained red with my blood. "It sure is bleeding a lot, though. Here. Hold this against your nose and put your head back."

I did as I was told.

"Do you think I can still play?"

The medic shrugged.

"That's up to you. I don't see any reason you can't continue with a little bit of protection."

"Protection?"

She showed me a mask designed to protect my hurt nose.

"I can't wear that! I'll look ridiculous!"

She shrugged.

"If you want to play, you have to wear the mask. It's the rules."

"Oh, man."

I took the mask from her and trudged back to our team. Everyone celebrated the win, nobody more than Coach Johnson. His smile was so big I was afraid his head would split in half.

"Why does Coach Johnson look so happy?" I asked Percival, who seemed to know those kind of things.

"At last year's tournament, the Cannons made it to the semifinals but were soundly defeated by Exeter. I suppose he takes it personal."

"I take it personal, too. My nose really hurts. I can't believe they didn't card that guy."

"Between you and me, the referees seem somewhat biased and play favorites."

I didn't like the sound of that. Coach Johnson got us together right about then, so I sort of stopped thinking about it. The idea that the refs were dirty stuck in the back of my mind, though.

"You guys did great today. Just don't let it go to your heads. You have the rest of the day off, but..."

We all started cheering. Coach Johnson blew his whistle until we quieted down.

"BUT you'd better spend your time in one of three places. Your rooms, the library so you can do your homework, or the stadium if you want to scout the competition. No leaving the campus under any circumstances. Understood?"

Percival's hand shot up.

"Sir! My parents are here to spectate. Surely, I may venture out with them."

Coach Johnson shrugged.

"If your parents are here to chaperone you, fine. But the rest of you, it's stadium, library, or room."

I already knew where I was going to spend my off-time. I got out my notebook and my pen and started scouting the other teams. I was running low on blank pages. Paul and I had gone over a lot in the last month.

The next game pitted La Forge against Picard. Right away, I saw a big difference in their play styles. La Forge constantly switched up their formations and tried tricky strategies to move the ball down the pitch.

By contrast, the Picard guys were totally by the book. Every play they made on the field was the "right" thing to do strategically. This made it easy to predict them, though.

La Forge was always one step ahead. I took some additional notes, mostly about the players on La Forge's side, because it was pretty obvious by the first half who was going to win. La Forge scored two goals to nothing.

When the game ended, La Forge won 4 to 0. It was downright embarrassing for the Picard team. I felt sorry for the players because the coaches kept going back to the same old strats and formations that clearly didn't work.

I wanted to scope out the rest of the competition. I was starving, though, and went to the dining hall for a late lunch. The food was a lot better because it was hot and fresh. Almost nobody was in the dining hall. Everyone seemed to be at the soccer stadium.

I did make it back to the stadium for the final match of the day, which was a game between two of the Western Conference teams. Jackson Academy wore green and gold, and man, could they play! The other team in black and white were pretty good, too, but nowhere near the level of the Jackson team.

I noticed a lot of green and gold in the stands. It looked like most of the players from Jackson had family in attendance. It made me miss my own family. I knew that my Mom and Dad couldn't make this tourney ahead of time. I thought I was okay with it.

But sitting there alone in that huge arena made me feel small again. I did my best, but I couldn't concentrate on my notes any longer. I left before the final Western Conference game was played.

After dinner, I found that Percival still hadn't returned to the room. Probably still out with his parents. I tried to imagine what his parents would be like. I kept picturing them as the King and Queen of England, even though Percival wasn't even British.

I should have been happy about winning the game against Exeter. But all it did was put more pressure on me. Now, we had to get past La Forge, a team that smoked their competition in the first tourney match.

The coaches hadn't let us bring cell phones on the trip, which was why Percival skirted the rules with his tablet. I really wanted to talk to my folks, but I didn't know their numbers, and there wasn't even a phone in the dorm room.

I wound up drifting off to sleep with an ice pack on my nose. Tomorrow would be grueling. I hoped I was up to the challenge.

CHAPTER 15

Yo, DJ, Kick It One More Time

"The only place success comes before hard work is the dictionary."

— Vince Lombardi

The sun barely peeked its face out when I arrived at the pitch the next morning. I spotted my team gathered on the bleachers. Even though I had left early, I was still one of the last to arrive.

The coaches stood together in a little huddle at the bottom of the bleachers, talking and occasionally looking out at our opponents for the next tournament bracket: La Forge Academy.

When most of the team arrived and sat down in the bleachers, Coach Johnson patted the other two coaches on the shoulder and turned to look at us.

"Good morning, Cannons. Welcome to the second day of the tournament."

He applauded, and after a second, the rest of us joined in.

"Congratulations on your victory yesterday, but that was the easy part. Today, we're facing arguably the best team in the tourney, La Forge Academy."

We all fell quiet. I nodded to myself. I pretty much had the same idea. La Forge was the best, maybe even better than us.

"We're playing on their home turf," Coach Bobby said, his rough voice like sandpaper. "The refs are all from around this area, so you know what that means."

Coach Stan stepped forward.

"That's why we're not going to leave it in the hands of the officials. We're going to play excellent, technical, back-breaking soccer today, so there's no doubt left in anyone's mind that we are the best."

The best? Were we really the best? Just the idea got my blood pumping. Maybe we were the best! We had a lot of good players, even Daniel, though I didn't like him very much as a person.

But the other team had their star players, too, Coach Johnson brought up.

"La Forge has some superstar players. Take their Center-Back, Rinaldo. He's the tall kid with the bushy hair and the birthmark on his knee."

I looked over, but I already knew who Coach was talking about. I'd taken note of him yesterday while watching the slaughter that was their game against Picard.

"Rinaldo steals passes," Coach Johnson said. "Beware of him. But defense isn't their only asset. They have a striker who is simply unbelievable."

"Number six, playing as four, Antonio Morales," I blurted.

Coach Johnson snapped his gaze up at me. I could have wilted like a dried out flower.

"Sorry," I said, hunching myself down in a vain attempt to hide.

"No, you're right. That's exactly who I was going to bring up." Coach Johnson jutted his clipboard toward the other team. "The short, skinny kid with a look on his face like he's better than all of us is Antonio. His leg speed is incredible, and he tends to sneak around defenders as a result."

Coach looked right at Percival.

"Percy, I'm counting on you to smother his behind. You feel me?"

"I'll do my best, coach. And it's Percival."

Coach Johnson snorted.

"That's what I said, isn't it? Now, let's go over some strategies for the game, and then we'll pick out our starting players."

My heart went thump thump thump in my chest. Was I going to be a starter at last? I thought I'd done pretty well yesterday, but I'd only been in the game for the last fifteen minutes of the second half.

I tried to pay attention to the strat session, but I kept thinking about the starting lineup. I really wanted to be a starter. It was a vote of confidence, something I could have really used right about then.

The coaches called the names for the starters. I sat up straight on the bleachers, shaking with anticipation but when they finished, my name wasn't one of those called.

I joined the other players on the bench, keeping my facial

mask hidden in the waistband of my shorts. I knew I looked ridiculous in it, but if I wanted to play I had to deal.

Pietro, Alex, and Han didn't make the starting lineup, either. I wondered at that since they'd all performed very well the previous day. The four of us sat together and tried to shout encouragement to our teammates. They were going to need it.

La Forge won the coin toss, but they elected to receive the kickoff. The ball flew through the air into their midst, and the game was on.

La Forge started out with a 4-3-3 formation. Their aggressive style clashed with our own 5-3-2, which focused on defense.

The La Forge Wingers put on a passing clinic. Every time I was sure they would have the ball tackled away from them, they passed to one another. But even as they ground to a halt against our defensive line, I saw someone flash up the pitch on the outskirts of both teams.

The striker, Antonio. He got right up on our goal, less than ten feet away, and waited. No one was paying any attention to him, not even our goaltender, Vince.

"Watch out for Antonio!" I shouted. "Number six! Somebody cover number six!"

With the roar of the crowd and everything, it was no wonder they didn't hear me. All I could do was look on helplessly as the La Forge right-winger shot Antonio a sneaky pass. Antonio caught the ball on his foot, bounced it several times in the air, and then smashed it toward our goal.

Vince dove for it, his chest smacking the ball. It rolled right into our net anyway because he hadn't been quite fast enough.

The air horn bleated, and the biased crowd went nuts. It was really scary, knowing that pretty much the entire arena was against us. La Forge had the benefit of the 12th man.

After the goal, things didn't get any better for our team. La Forge kept possession of the ball for most of the first half. Our guys managed to keep them from scoring again, but only just barely. Only a handful of times was the ball even on the La Forge side of the pitch.

I kept wondering why the coaches were using purely defensive formations. Obviously, we couldn't win that way. Defensive formations were good for creating chances at a counter attack, but La Forge just wouldn't let that happen.

At halftime, the coaches got together in their little huddle again. From time to time, one of them would look over at our bench. I tried not to show it, but I really hoped they were about to put me in.

"All right," Coach Johnson shouted "Robbie, Dwayne, Richard, and Daniel, hit the bench. Alex, Han, Pietro, and Goalman, you're in."

I got up and jogged toward the pitch. Coach Bobby got in my way.

"Uh uh, Max. I spoke to the medic. You have to wear your protective gear."

I grimaced but I was too excited to get on the field to argue. I slipped the elastic band around the back of my head and put on the mask.

Coach Bobby laughed.

"It's the Phantom of the Opera," he said. I have no idea what he was talking about. I've never even been to the opera, and why would a phantom need a mask?

"Don't let it bother you, Max," Pietro said, grabbing me by the elbow. "You look great. Like a superhero or something."

"Really?" I asked.

"No, not really you look like a dork, but who cares? It only matters how you play."

I grimaced behind my mask, but he was right about the dork part and the playing part.

They set us up on a 4-3-3 formation. An attacking formation at last! I knew it fell onto us to get the ball into the goal, and the La Forge players would not make it easy.

We received the kickoff. The ball came right for me, and I intercepted, dribbling up the pitch. La Forge stuck to their own 4-3-3 strategy, which gave us the numbers advantage on their half of the field.

Two fullbacks converged on my position. Talk about being between a rock and a hard place! I knew they could tackle me, working together. So I didn't give them a chance.

I swept my leg laterally across my body, passing the ball through a hole in their defenses to Han. He dribbled the ball diagonally toward their goal, La Forge's defenders in hot pursuit. I jogged up behind the crowd, waiting and watching for an opportunity.

My opportunity came when one of the La Forge fullbacks went for a slide tackle. He got the better of Han, sending the ball out of reach. It would have gone out of bounds, but I raced up and caught it.

I dribbled the ball toward the goal. It was so close now! But two of the defenders were still on their feet and rushing to intercept me. I looked, but I had no good passing opportunities.

I had to take the shot myself, but first, I had to get past

the two defenders. Inspiration struck me. All that time practicing with Paul was about to pay off.

As they got to within mere feet of me, I used my heel to kick the ball behind me. I bounced it off the back of my shoe and sent it into the air in a perfect Rainbow.

The fullbacks slammed into me, almost knocking me over. But they were focused behind me, where they thought I'd sent the ball in a rear pass.

I staggered forward and regained my balance just in time to intercept the ball and dribble it forward. The goaltender's eyes were focused on the mass of boys fifteen feet away. He hadn't seen my rainbow trick, either.

When I took my shot, he finally noticed. The goaltender jumped, hands just missing the ball as it sank into the net.

Everyone else on my team shouted and cheered. I wanted to, but for some reason, I almost collapsed. It was such a relief to have scored the goal! Now, I had definitely proven myself.

But would it put me in the starting lineup?

"Good job, Goalman," hollered Coach Bobby, of all people. "That was a highlight reel moment!"

Han came up and whopped me on the shoulder blades so hard he almost knocked me over. Then Alex grabbed my arm and raised it in the air...only he was taller than me, so my feet came off the ground!

"Ow! Okay, back off already!"

"Sorry," Alex said.

We reached back to our half of the pitch. Coach Johnson called for a defensive 5-3-2 formation. I thought that was a good idea since the La Forge players were ticked off! We were the first team to score a goal on them in the tourney in three years, I later found out.

At the time, though, they looked like they wanted to murder us, and I didn't know why. I faced off with their striker, Antonio. He had possession and looked as if he wanted to get into scoring position.

I didn't want to let that happen. I went in for the tackle, remembering what Coach Johnson told me all those months ago. I kept my body over the ball, planting my foot on the opposite side.

We dueled over the ball, our feet flashing around like crazy. Man, his legs were quick! Antonio nearly got the better of me, but I think because I'd sat out the first half, I had a little more gas in the tank.

The ball squirted out between us and bounced crazily across the grass. Both teams went for it, hard. Bodies crashed into bodies, and dust rose into the air, making it hard to see.

I tried to get into the thick of it, but the refs started blaring on their whistles. Someone got a yellow card.

It turned out to be Percival.

"I didn't mean to," Percival said, looking very upset as the medics worked on one of the La Forge players. "He tripped and fell, and I hit him with my knee. It was an accident."

"It happens, Percival," I said. "Don't dwell on it."

My dad said that to me a lot. Don't dwell on it. I didn't quite understand what he meant, but it sounded good coming out of my mouth.

"Don't dwell on it?" Percival sputtered. "Maxwell, you realize what this means? They're going to get a penalty kick!"

"So?" I said. "Vince has super-glue on his fingertips."

"You didn't notice, but Coach Johnson swapped out Vince for Gabriel."

My heart sank. Gabriel had yet to play in the tournament, and with good reason. The only position he could play was goaltender, and he wasn't that good at it.

"If they get the penalty kick, they take the advantage. And there isn't much time left on the clock."

He was right. All we could do was line up and watch as Antonio set himself up for the penalty kick. Gabriel's freckled face looked pretty scared. I would have been scared, too.

"You've got this, Gabe," I shouted. Somehow, I made it sound like I believed it.

My words were like magic. Gabriel stopped looking so scared. Instead, he looked determined! All of a sudden, I felt better about our chances.

Antonio rushed up on the ball, his legs moving in a blur. He grunted right before his foot made contact with the ball. He put so much English on the soccer ball it twisted in the air like a top. Gabriel side jumped, his arms and legs splayed wide.

I cringed as the ball shot toward the air right over his head. Gabe jumped up, his arms outstretched...

And caught the ball right in the face.

The crowd, the players on both teams and even the coaches gave a collective "ooooh" as Gabriel crumpled to the grass. But he landed with his left arm still trapping the ball, stained red with his blood.

A moment later, Gabriel sat bolt upright like the Undertaker, and then shoved the ball in the air and shouted. The crowd erupted in cheers. Even though they were biased for La Forge, it was hard not to root for Gabriel after that play.

"You see, Percival? You were worried about nothing."

"Perhaps," Percival said with a snort.

They swapped Gabriel out with Robert, which relieved me despite what I'd told Percival. The game was far from over. Coach Johnson switched up our strategy to 3-5-2. Instead of scoring, we were supposed to focus on keeping possession of the ball.

"It's Park the Bus all over again," I said, mostly to myself as we gathered on our half of the pitch for the throw-in. "But we're not in the lead. It's tied up."

"I'm sure Rex Rocket knows what he's doing," Daniel said with a sneer. He'd just been put back in the game, replacing Alex as our left-winger. "If you ask me, Park the Bus is a tactic for losers, though."

"Oh yeah? It sure helped us beat your Jericho Junior High behind back home!"

He loomed over me, his face twisted up and angry.

CHAPTER 16

Not in Kansas Anymore, Toto

"Everything is funny, as long as it's happening to somebody else."

— Will Rogers

"We're not back home anymore! This is the big leagues, Goalman. Are you sure you belong here?"

"I know I belong here!" I shot back. Our chests were touching, and I fought the urge to hit him.

"Oh yeah? Then how come you haven't started a single game this tourney?"

I was about to hit him when the refs blared on their whistles.

"Cannon coaches, get control of your team," shouted one of the refs.

"You two knock it off," Coach Johnson said, "or you're both benched."

We backed away from each other, acting like angry cats.

The throw-in went to La Forge. Their center immediately dribbled the ball toward our goal. Daniel and I both went in for the tackle. At the last second, I gave it to him and instead positioned myself on the outside of the mob.

Daniel and the center fought over possession of the ball. Daniel got the better of him after a furious round of footwork. His eyes caught me, and then he sent the ball my way.

I dribbled the ball laterally, keeping out of reach of the attacking La Forge players. Their aggressive strategy gave them the advantage so long as we remained on our half of the pitch.

Alex was in position to my left. I passed to him just as a La Forge winger came in for a tackle. I got caught up in his legs, and we both tripped. I was glad I had the mask on because his shoulder slammed into my face. It still hurt, even with the mask, but I can only imagine it would have been a lot worse.

Maybe it wasn't so bad to look like a dork.

I threw myself to my feet, ignoring the pain in my face, and searched for the ball. Our team had worked it onto their half of the field. Our passing game kept the La Forge team scrambling to get possession of the ball.

The strategy was working, but I didn't know what the coaches were thinking. If they ran out the game clock, the game would end in a tie. In normal season play, it would have been the end of things, neither team winning.

In a tourney, however, there would be ten more minutes of overtime. Running out the clock didn't seem to get us anything.

The clock ticked down, and we were able to smother La

Forge. When there was only two minutes left, Coach called for a time-out. The refs granted it.

Those of us left on the field jogged over to him, all of us breathing hard. It had been a brutal game, and my legs felt like rubber.

"All right, Cannons," Coach Johnson growled. "This is it. No more running out the clock. We're switching it up to 4-3-3. You score me a goal at all costs!"

Score? He wanted us to score with two minutes left on the clock? It wasn't impossible, but that didn't make it easy.

With our team focused on offense, we had the numbers advantage on their half of the pitch. Alex and I passed and dribbled the ball, weaving our way through the La Forge defensive line. A huge player loomed in front of me, like a living mountain. He went for the tackle, but I slid through the grass and punted the ball to Alex.

He took possession and dribbled back toward our edge of the pitch. Coach Johnson hollered for us to score. At the moment, we were struggling to even keep the ball away from La Forge.

Alex fought for possession of the ball with a La Forge defender. Suddenly, the La Forge fullback stumbled. To keep his balance, he grabbed Alex's jersey.

The refs blew their whistles like mad. The offending player got a yellow card, and Alex got a free kick.

Alex ran up on the ball and smacked it so hard I could feel it in my stomach. The ball spun like crazy through the air, bouncing off the grassy pitch and heading toward the enemy goal. La Forge's goalkeeper launched himself in the air and snatched up the ball as easy as breathing.

My heart sank, but the game wasn't over. Not yet. I checked the game clock. Under a minute! How were we supposed score with so little time?

I shook off the bad attitude. Coach wanted us to score. It was up to us now.

"Come on, guys," I shouted, trying to rally our offensive formation. "We've got this! They're getting tired!"

"Shut up, Goalman," Daniel snapped. "Just get me the ball that's all you have to do."

The La Forge goaltender passed the ball back into play. Alex, Daniel, and I worked together, confusing the dribbling La Forge halfback. I went in for a hard slide tackle and smacked the ball away from him.

Back and forth, we battled on their half of the pitch. Every time we managed to get the ball, La Forge found a way to steal it back. My jersey stuck to my body with sweat. I heaved and panted, dragging air into my tired body but I didn't give up.

Finally, with less than thirty seconds on the clock, we made a hard push for their goal. Our attackers swarmed the defending players. I had possession, dribbling for the goal. I passed to Daniel, expecting him to pass to Alex, who was in a better scoring position.

Instead, Daniel hogged the ball, just like he did in the park back home. He went for the goal kick himself. The La Forge goaltender clapped the ball to his chest. The crowd roared. We all braced ourselves for the throw-in.

The goaltender surprised us. He snapped his foot forward and kicked the ball high over our heads. It bounced onto our half of the pitch — where Antonio was waiting.

He intercepted the ball and dribbled toward our goal.

"No!" I shouted. "Stop him!"

"Way to hog the ball, Daniel," Percival growled.

Daniel looked sheepish. It didn't matter to me how he felt.

What mattered was stopping the enemy striker before he could get a goal.

Daniel stretched his super long legs out. He ate up the terrain like a starving giant. I was amazed that he caught up with Antonio.

The two of them fought for possession of the ball. Tackles, counter tackles, and lots of body contact resulted in a stalemate.

But I reached them right about then. I hooked the ball with my toes and snagged it out of their dueling legs.

Dribbling like mad, I returned the ball to their half of the pitch. I kept my eyes on the opposition, my own players, and my coaches in case they gave a signal. Both teams bunched up near the goal.

Alex and Han covered the fullbacks, letting me dribble right between them. The goaltender was ready for me, but I wasn't going to take the shot anyway.

I kicked the ball over to Pietro, who ran for the goal. He looked all the world like he was going to try and smash it in past the goaltender using brute force.

But then he flicked the ball behind him in a rear pass, where Alex caught it. I intercepted a fullback before he could tackle the ball from Alex.

Alex took his shot. The ball spun through the air. La Forge's goaltender stretched out his arms. I held my breath.

The ball smacked into the goaltender's fingertips, then continued on until it struck the net. Oh, what a sweet sound that was!

The air horn went off, and when I checked the lock we had one second remaining. No way would they be able to score in one second.

When we did the kickoff, the other team just half-heartedly jogged until the buzzer sounded. The Cannons celebrated our victory. We'd beat the toughest team in the tournament!

At a cost, though. When the adrenaline wore off, I realized how tired I was and how much my legs hurt. I wasn't the only one, either. Most of us could barely sit up straight for the post-game rally.

"You all made me proud today," Coach Johnson said. Then his smile faded, and he glared right at Daniel. "But remember, there is no I in team!"

Coach Johnson warned us again not to leave campus during our off hours. As we shuffled away from the bleachers, all of us super tired. Coach Stan waved me over.

"Goalman, you need to visit the medic."

"What? Why? My face hurts a little, but it's fine."

His nose twitched.

"Take off your mask."

I had forgotten I still had the thing on. I slipped it off, and my face started to throb right away. When I looked at the mask, the inside was covered in blood. My blood.

"Medic. Now."

I fought off a wave of panic. If the medics decided I was too hurt to play, I would have to sit out the third and final game our team would play in the tournament.

The same pretty lady who had helped me yesterday saw me walking up to her. I looked at her name badge. "Tran." I resolved to remember her name.

"Oh my goodness," she said as I got closer. "Your face is a mess again. Did you take another hit?"

"Yeah, but the mask protected me."

"Not enough, it seems. Sit down and let me take a look."

Tran cleaned me up with a cotton swab and then pressed her gloved fingers against my face. I winced and even cried out as she probed around. How come doctors always have to do stuff that hurts when you're already hurt?

"Hmm," she said. I didn't like the way she said it.

"What?" I sputtered. "I'm good to play, right?"

"I don't know, Max. Yesterday, I thought the main problem was your nose. Now, I'm starting to worry you have a hairline fracture of your cheekbone."

I put my hand to my face. It did kind of hurt really bad in that one spot when I touched it too hard.

"Um, I don't think it's that bad," I lied.

"Max, I really think you should sit the last game out."

"No!"

I blinked away tears.

"Please, let me play! I'll wear the mask and I'll be careful, I promise."

Tran sighed.

"All right. I'm going to take your word for it, Max. But if the pain suddenly gets worse, or your nose starts bleeding again for no reason, you tell me or another medic right away. You hear me?"

I bobbed my head up and down, feeling super grateful.

"Thank you! Thank you, thank you so much!"

Her face got all stern.

"I mean it, Max. You could get me in trouble if you're hurt worse than you're letting on."

That made me feel guilty. But I also knew I could still play.

"I know you mean it! I'll be careful, and if it gets worse, I promise I'll go to the doctor."

She gave me one last look to make sure I knew she meant it. Then she nodded and sent me on my way with a new, clean protective mask.

After dinner, I fell into a super deep sleep. I didn't wake up until well after midnight. Then, I only stayed awake long enough to use the bathroom and drink about three bottles of water before going back to bed.

The next morning, I woke up to Percival's alarm and an aching face. I looked at myself in the mirror. My face was all puffy and swollen, but on the inside, I felt amazing.

One more game to go. We would be facing the winner of the Western Conference, Jackson Academy.

I wondered if I would be put in the starting lineup or not. But another part of me started to think it didn't matter so much. I was finding ways to contribute to the team. Not only that, I was finding ways to shine.

Sooner or later, my hard work would pay off. I had to keep believing that. My mom, my dad, my sister, and even my coaches were all rooting for me. I didn't want to let them all down.

When we got to the stadium, there was a different feel to it all. Everyone on both teams was real quiet. I felt the weight of the whole tourney bearing down on me. It was like being crushed under a planet.

"Hey, what happened?" Coach Johnson snapped. "I came here to coach the Cannons. I don't recognize all of these mopey, scared-looking little boys wearing team uniforms."

We all kind of looked at each other. Even the normally confident Percival seemed subdued.

"Well? Where's my team?"

"Here," about half of us mumbled.

"I can't hear you!"

"Here!" we said, a little louder.

"I said I can't hear you. Where's my team?"

"Here!"

I yelled, my throat raw, and so did everyone else. My heart thundered in my chest. Blood swept through my body. Now, I wanted to do nothing else than get on the pitch and play some serious soccer.

"That's better," Coach Johnson roared. "Okay, here's our strategy. Jackson Academy has a deep, deep roster. But they have three players that stand out."

Coach Johnson looked over at Coach Stan.

"Oh, you want me to do it? Okay."

Stan cleared his throat and stepped forward.

"Number ten, playing as number ten, Domingo. This guy never gets tired, and he helps his team score."

Stan showed us some footage of Domingo in action. He was a thick-bodied but fast kid with phenomenal footwork. One thing was for sure: Domingo didn't hog the ball. Most of the highlights Coach Stan showed us involved Domingo with the assist rather than the goal.

"Next up is Gunter, number four, playing as number

nine. This kid has a pituitary disorder or something. He's just huge."

The footage he showed us featured a tall, lanky kid who ran even faster than Alberto from the La Forge team. A lot of the time he won tackles because his legs were just so much longer than his opponent's. Not that he wasn't good. He really was. But his height gave him a definite edge.

"Finally, number five playing as number one, the goalkeeper, Noah. This kid has sticky hands like a fly."

Noah snatched balls out of the air like a frog catching flies. I could see he would be tough to score on.

"We've played two hard games of soccer," Coach Johnson said. "But this is going to be the hardest of all. We're not holding back until the second half this time. We're going all out from the get-go."

Coach Johnson flipped open his clipboard and started reading names. I promised myself I wouldn't freak out as he read the names of the starting lineup. I broke my promise with myself pretty quick. I knew that being on the starting lineup wasn't the be all and end all of soccer.

But man, did I want it! I wanted it so bad I could taste it.

I was so worked up it didn't register when Coach Johnson called my name. When I did let it sink in, I almost fainted with happiness. Finally, I'd made it. Then Coach Johnson told me my position.

"Sweeper."

I wasn't in my usual position of attacking midfielder.

"You want me to sweep, coach?" I asked Coach Johnson. "That's not my normal position."

"True, but I need you to clean up any balls that make it

across the backline. You might still get to be an attacker, but right now, I need you here."

I didn't argue. I knew that the best players were the most flexible players. Even Messi didn't play just one position.

It still kind of bothered me to watch the offensive players rush across the pitch while I had to hang back. I knew I had an important role, but it still felt like I was on the sidelines watching the game.

Our 4-3-3 formation pressed the Jackson defensive players, but we couldn't seem to get in scoring position.

Their midfielder, Domingo, got possession of the ball and dribbled down the pitch. I swept along the backline to intercept him, joined by Percival. We moved in sync, blocking the path of Domingo and making him veer off.

Alex tackled the ball away from him in the middle of a press. For a second, I couldn't see the ball at all; just a lot of scrambling bodies.

Then, I noticed the ball bouncing away all by itself. No one else was on it, so I tore my cleats across the grass. I took possession and dribbled slowly toward the enemy half of the field, looking for a teammate to pass to.

Nobody was open except Daniel. I shot him the ball, hoping he wouldn't hog it and ruin things again.

Daniel dribbled toward the goal, but two fullbacks converged to tackle. He juked them, spinning around in a half circle while keeping the ball bouncing in the air off his kicking feet.

Then he swatted the ball with the side of his foot. Han took possession and raced toward the enemy goal.

Han lined up his shot, and it was a thing of beauty. I could hear the whiff whiff whiff of the ball as it spun through the air. That was how hard he'd kicked it.

But Noah sprang up into the air like he had springs for legs. He snatched the ball out of the air and landed, clutching it to his chest.

We all got real careful, watching him closely. He faked out a kick and instead tossed the ball to one of his teammates.

I watched, feeling helpless as our offensive players struggled to get and keep possession of the ball. Being a defensive player was not my cup of tea, as my mom would say. I didn't know how Percival could stand it.

We played to win, and so did they. But when the air horn went off to signal the end of the first half, neither of us had scored a goal.

Coach Johnson rallied us to the bench. His face was bright red, both from yelling out instructions to us and from running up and down the pitch to follow the action.

"All right, don't get frustrated, Cannons," he growled. "They're smothering our offense, but they haven't managed to score, either. We still have the second half to make the magic happen. That's why I'm switching up the lineup."

I felt a little dismayed that I was taken off the field, but so were most of the starting lineup. I sat on the bench and longed to be back on the field. That didn't mean I wasn't super supportive of my team. I cheered for them so loud my throat hurt.

My throat wasn't the only thing that hurt, though. My face had started to throb about ten minutes into the first half.

Now the protective mask felt uncomfortably tight. I knew if I took it off, though, the coaches would get a look at my face and send me to the medics. I didn't want to get taken out of the game for good.

Coach Johnson shuffled us up. To my surprise, he moved

Percival up to center. Percival looked like he wanted to argue, but one look from Coach Bobby shut him down.

Daniel got pushed back to sweeper, and Alex came in as the Winger. I waited, hoping Coach Johnson wasn't going to bench me. He'd replaced me as a sweeper, after all.

"Goalman," Coach Johnson snapped without looking up from his tablet. "You think you can manage number ten?"

I blinked in confusion as it sank in.

"Attacking midfielder? You bet I can manage it!"

"All right. Pick your striker."

My stomach churned because I knew the right answer was also the one I least wanted to say.

"Daniel," I said at last.

"What? Daniel is your sweeper."

"Yeah, but he'd make a better striker. Han can sweep up the balls for us."

Coach Johnson stared into me so hard I thought I would come apart. But then he nodded.

"All right. Han, you're in, Daniel, you've got about thirty seconds of time-out left to work out a strat with your team. Make it count."

Daniel glared at me as he drew nearer.

"What's the big idea, Goalman? You expect me to be grateful or something?"

"No," I snapped, getting up in his face. "I expect you to play like you're on a team! Work with us, and we can make magic happen."

"Yes, Daniel, don't be obtuse," Percival chimed in. "We can overwhelm their defense if we work together, and you remember that passing the ball is an option."

"You sure about this, Mr. Snoogie?" Alex asked. "I could take over as striker."

"Daniel can do it."

"Yeah, but will he?"

We all turned to look at Daniel as the refs blew the whistle, indicating the time-out was over. He nodded.

"Yeah. Yeah, I'll do what's best for the team."

I hoped I was right about him. I felt like Daniel was our strongest offensive player and would be wasted at midfield sweeping up balls.

But if I was wrong, and he chose to go off on his own again, we'd lose this game and any chance we had of making it into the finals.

We jogged onto the pitch. The sun blazed down overhead, sizzling my skin and making the air hot and hard to breathe. Percival shot me a look that said it all. We still had an entire half to play, and things were already brutal.

A mad scramble at kickoff led to the ball going out of bounds. Jackson's corner got the throw-in on their side of the pitch. Coach Johnson had us set for a 4-3-3 formation, to play an attacking style. But Jackson's defensive posture had them outnumbering us anyway.

Just like in the park back home, though, we could use their extra man to our advantage. If we could pull together as a team.

The throw-in put the ball in possession of Jackson's attacking midfielder. He only got about ten feet onto our half of the pitch when Han snuck up and slide-tackled it away from him.

Since they were closest, Alex and Daniel moved in first. Alex fought off two deafening Jackson players, heel-passing the ball to Daniel.

He dribbled for the goal. I kept pace, along with Percival. The two fullbacks reared up between us and Daniel, like a living wall.

I caught Percival's gaze, and once I knew I had his attention, I cut sharply to my left, moving diagonally along the pitch. I fell behind Daniel and the Jackson defensive mob.

Daniel had no chance of getting close enough to take his shot. He had to know it. My stomach did flip-flops as the Jackson players hemmed him in tighter and tighter.

Percival moved into position behind the mob of players. Alex tried to block for Daniel. His legs got tangled up with the Jackson sweeper, and they both went down in a gruesome heap.

Daniel had no one close by. His eyes darted around, then centered on Percival. Just when three Jackson defenders were about to tackle, Daniel passed the ball back toward our half of the pitch.

Percival took possession, smoothly dribbling diagonally. The Jackson players moved to intercept, thinking he was going for the goal himself.

But Percival sneak-passed to me instead. I dribbled to the left side, running free and clear of any defenders.

I had time to line up my shot. But their goaltender was looking right at me. He knew it was coming. I had to do more than be accurate. I had to be tricky.

It was all wrong to set up a Rainbow. So I reached back into the bag of tricks I used at the old park. I drew my leg back and tried to make it look like I was going to shoot for the right side of the goal.

I missed the ball, my cleats passing over the leather. The goalkeeper took the bait, leaping to the right.

I spun around in a tight circle, using my left leg as a pivot. At the end of my spin, I stuck my right foot out and kicked the ball, this time for real.

I sent the ball behind me to a waiting Daniel. He kicked the ball in the empty space the goaltender had just left behind him.

The goaltender's eyes went wide. He knew he'd been had. Scrambling like crazy, he tried to throw himself in front of the ball, but it sailed past his fingers by mere inches.

I'd never heard a sweeter sound than the ball hitting the net. The crowd erupted with cheers. I just kept staring at the ball, not believing we'd actually scored the game's first goal.

"Great job, Maxwell," Percival said, his face red and shining with sweat. "Your plan worked to perfection."

"Only because they expected Daniel to hog the ball. It won't work twice."

Daniel and Alex raced up to join us as we jogged up the pitch. Coach Johnson switched us to a 5-3-2 formation, leaving Daniel and me as the sole offensive players.

"He's Parking the Bus," Daniel griped. "Just like you did in Jericho park."

"It's not a bad strategy," I said. "I mean, we have the lead."

"We should try to expand on the lead and score more points."

"You just want to score a goal because I did," I snapped.

He grinned.

"Of course I do. But I'm not wrong, either. The best defense is a good offense."

We remained on their half of the pitch while our defensive line stifled Jackson's every attempt to score. They came close, though, more than once.

Time seemed to take forever to tick down on the game clock. I was getting worried. If we couldn't run out the clock before they scored, our strategy would backfire. They could at least tie us up.

And if Jackson got the advantage and scored another goal, then we wouldn't have time to rally.

Things got really hot on our half of the pitch. A seven-player pileup occurred right near the goal. I couldn't even see what started it, but the refs decided that a Jackson player was at fault and gave him a yellow card.

"Penalty kick," I said excitedly, grabbing Daniel's jersey. "This could be our chance."

"I doubt that. Look who our kicker is."

Percival trotted up. I didn't want to bad mouth my friend. I still worried just as much as Daniel. Percival was an excellent player, but his goal shots were always predictable.

"Maybe he'll surprise us," I said out of the corner of my mouth.

CHAPTER 17

The Grass is Always Greener on the Other Side of the Septic Tank

"I always wanted to be somebody, but now I realize I should have been more specific."

— Lily Tomlin

D aniel snorted.

"Quit trying to be positive about everything, Mr. Snoogie. You're not a coach."

"It's better than always being negative! Maybe have some faith in our team."

Daniel turned a smirk my way.

"Okay, Goalman. Let's make a bet."

"My mom says I'm not supposed to gamble."

He rolled his eyes while we lined up for the penalty kick.

"Are you a mama's boy, Mr. Snoogie?"

I knew he was just trying to get me mad, so I'd say yes

to his bet. But it worked. I was that worked up, I guess.

"No, I'm not a mama's boy. What's the bet?"

"If Percy Jackson, the donut thief here can kick the goal, then I'll admit I should be nicer to everyone. But if he misses, you have to admit that Percy sucks at kicking goals. Not to me, but to him."

I ground my teeth in frustration.

"All right, you're on."

Even when the words left my mouth, I knew I'd made a mistake. Percival walked up to the ball, wearing a look of supreme concentration. He was going to kick it as hard and as fast as he could, right up the middle, and the goaltender would catch it.

He jogged a few steps back and blew out a sigh. Then he took his run, and I clenched up...

Percival stopped and then turned his back on the ball.

"I can't do it! I can't!"

Daniel burst into laughter while I looked on in shock.

"Percival, you kick that ball!" coach Bobby screamed from the sidelines.

"What happens if he doesn't take the shot?" Han muttered.

I didn't know, myself. I'd never seen anyone not take their penalty kick before. No one else seemed to know what to do, either. Even the refs stood around looking confused.

Someone in the crowd started to boo. It picked up and carried across the whole audience. Percival sank into a crouch and covered his ears with his hands.

All of a sudden, I was jogging over to him. I didn't even

think about it. I just knew it needed to be done.

"Percival, what's wrong?"

"I can't do it, Maxwell. Everyone knows I'm going to miss. Everyone."

"That's not true."

"Yes, it is. I'm just not good at kicking goals."

"You can do it, Percival. I believe in you."

I looked over at Daniel and glared at him.

"We all do, don't we, Daniel?"

This was it. If Daniel were ever going to be a team player, this is when he needed to step up. For a second, I could see the smart mouth remark in his eyes.

But then, he started clapping.

"Yeah, you can do it, Percy! Kick that ball right down that Jackson goaltending punk's throat!"

Pretty soon, all of our team clapped for Percival. He stood up and took a deep breath through his nostrils.

"All right, Maxwell. I'll do it. Perhaps I can't be as fancy as your double foot sweep, but I'll do my best."

"You've got this."

I jogged back to the line.

"Thanks, Daniel."

"Don't mention it, Mr. Snoogie. Of course, now it's going to be extra humiliating for Percy if he misses the shot."

I gritted my teeth but didn't respond. Mom says there are some people who just turn around everything you say to them. I think Daniel fits that category.

Percival blew air out of his mouth, puffing up his cheeks like balloons. He squinted in the bright sunlight, focused on the black and white ball.

I held my breath as Percival began his run. The smack of his foot into the leather echoed in my ears. I watched as the ball shot toward the upper left corner of the goal.

The Jackson goaltender dashed madly for the save. He jumped, hands outstretched. The ball smacked into his palms, slowing but not quite stopping.

The goaltender fell to the grass as the ball struck the net. Percival stared at the ball inside of the net as if he didn't really believe it.

"You were right, Mr. Snoogie," Daniel said, shaking his head.

"Yeah, so long as you remember that your name from now on is Mr. Positive."

Daniel shrugged.

"A bet's a bet, and a real man never welches. I'll be a Pollyanna like you."

"You'll be a what?"

He sneered at me.

"Try picking up a book that isn't about soccer once in a while."

He jogged off to our half of the pitch. After a moment, I joined him. The coaches switched up our formation to 4-3-3, meaning we had plenty of attacking players. I didn't know if it was a good idea or not. The Jackson team looked pretty fired up after losing two goals in a row.

Sure enough, they knocked the ball deep into our pitch and

came at us with an all-out assault. Only their fullbacks remained on their half of the pitch.

"Stay mobile," I cried, shoving Alex and Daniel toward the right side of the pitch. "Look for chances to steal and score."

"Shouldn't we try to defend?" Alex asked.

"No way, look at those guys! They're going to get this goal or die trying. It's better to step aside and let the charging bull go past us."

I was rather proud of that charging bull line. But it didn't seem to work. Daniel and Alex listened to me, but Percival remained determined to join the defensive efforts.

Jackson's midfielder pulled off a sneaky pass, kicking the ball behind himself to their striker. I wasn't surprised when I saw the ball smack into our net: disappointed but not surprised.

"You were right, Goalman," Daniel said. "What do we do now?"

"We take possession of the ball and try to score again. They spent themselves pretty good on that last play."

"Yeah," Alex said. "They do look pretty tired."

They weren't the only ones. My legs felt like lead weights. I tried not to let it slow me down, but I was approaching the gassed-out zone.

Jackson kicked the ball so deep our goaltender caught it and threw it back into play. All of the Cannon team remained on our half of the pitch when their offensive line swarmed in. I did my best, but I lost sight of the ball. I tried to get in, but a huge mosh pit had formed in the center of the field.

Then I spotted the ball squirting out from a dozen kicking legs. I ran toward it, angling myself for an intercept to take possession.

Jackson's center popped out of the mob, and he was a lot closer to the ball than me. I knew he was going to get it. I changed my direction again so I could come up beside him and hopefully tackle the ball away.

Then Daniel just kind of appeared out of nowhere. His shoulder caught the Jackson Center right in the gut. The center doubled over as Daniel shoved him away.

Whistles blasted. A ref raced up and threw a red card in Daniel's face.

"You're out!"

My jaw fell open. A red card? Daniel had just been ejected from the game — and we weren't allowed to replace him.

"It was an accident," Daniel tried to argue, but no one was buying it. Even our own team knew Daniel had committed a blatant foul.

"You had to make him our winger, didn't you?" Alex said bitterly.

"I think he just got carried away," I said. Daniel did look absolutely miserable as he left the field. "We've got to turn this around."

We lined up for the Jackson penalty kick. Vince crouched low in our goal, ready to defend. The Jackson player Daniel had speared stepped up for the kick. I could tell he was hurting.

"Do you think he'll make the goal?" Percival asked.

"I don't know. He's hurt. He'll either let his pain make him miss the shot or..."

"Or what?"

I sighed.

"Or, he'll use it as motivation and kick like the world is ending."

As the Jackson player raced up, I could tell it was going to be option number two. He cracked that ball like a thunderbolt. Vince was ready and in the right position, but he wasn't quite fast enough.

"One more goal, and they even the score," Percival groaned.

"Then we can't let them have it."

"They have the numbers advantage," Han said.

"That doesn't mean it's over."

I ran over to Coach Johnson as the refs retrieved the ball. He glared down at me.

"Don't get us an offsides penalty, Max."

"Coach, we need to go on the offensive."

"We have the advantage. We need to focus on defense."

I shook my head.

"They have more players on the pitch than us. Coach Johnson, please, I've been in this situation before. They're going to be playing heavy offense. Their goal will be pretty much undefended."

Coach Johnson snorted.

"All right, Goalman. We'll do it your way. Don't disappoint me."

His words felt like a lead weight in my heart. Disappointing him was something I dreaded. Not to mention, I would disappoint my parents, my sister, and everyone from the old neighborhood, too.

But most of all, I would disappoint myself. I wanted to make the finals. I wanted the Cannons to win the tournament.

I wanted it so bad I could taste it.

"Okay, guys, we're going all out. Han, can you step up and take Daniel's place?"

He nodded.

"Sure, but is Coach okay with this?"

"Yes, he is."

The kickoff put the ball just on their side of the pitch. Both teams raced to take possession. Alex dove in and pulled off a beautiful slide tackle, his cleats trimming bits of grass as he sliced through the field.

The ball bounced crazy. I jumped up and smacked it with my forehead, bouncing it right to Han. Han dribbled toward the Jackson goal, zipping past the entire crowd of players on both sides.

Percival ran interference for him, fending off one of the Jackson fullbacks. Alex had regained his feet and now ran a few paces behind me. I angled off to the right, hoping he would get the hint of what I wanted him to do.

He did, breaking to the left. We each avoided the four-way pileup between the Jackson fullbacks, Percival, and Han.

Han saw that we were in position. He passed the ball to Alex. He let out a grunt and smashed the ball with his foot. The Jackson goaltender jumped up and blocked, the ball bouncing first off his chest, then his arm, and then his face.

The ball bounced out of the goal, spinning crazily through the grass. I jumped over the flailing legs of the Jackson sweeper, and mule kicked the ball back over to Alex.

Alex kicked the ball, his foot winding up in the air near his shoulder. The Jackson goaltender could only watch as the ball zipped past him and hit the net.

I grinned as we ran back to our half of the field. My legs felt like thin rubber bands, and every breath I took felt like I had an elephant grabbing my chest with its trunk.

We now had a two-point advantage. The tiny amount of time remaining on the clock took the fight out of Jackson. They ran after the ball, but nobody thought they had a chance of winning — not even them.

The buzzer blasted, signaling the end of the game. I went on wobbly legs toward the sidelines, where I could sit down and drink a gallon of Gatorade.

Everything broke open for me during that game against Jackson. From that point on, I felt like I was finally on the right path.

But if I thought that meant things were going to get easier, I was wrong. Dead wrong.

CHAPTER 18

When the Going Gets Tough, The Wise Seek Help

"I love me some me."

— Terrell Owens

The coaches took us out to a steakhouse as a reward for our victory. As hungry as I was, I actually would have rather eaten at the commissary and then crashed in my temporary bunk.

As it was, I barely stayed awake until dessert. Coach told us we'd be gathering at the stadium at 10 a.m. sharp.

That woke me up.

"But the final match isn't until one," someone complained.

"I said what I said." Coach Johnson glared us all down. "Be there at ten if you want a chance to play in the final. Period."

I don't know why anyone was worried. Half the bus was asleep before we even made it back to La Forge.

The long trudge from the bus to my temporary bunk couldn't get over with fast enough. I plopped down in the bed face down without even bothering to turn out the lights.

My dreams betrayed me. I kept trying to get to the soccer field, but there was always something in the way. Either a fence so high I couldn't climb it or a wide river with no bridge. My dreams didn't have to make any sense.

I came awake in a cold sweat, panicking because the sun was already up. I checked the time and found that I still had another hour before my alarm was set to go off. Percival continued to snore. I wished I could sleep that sound.

I really wished that my family could have seen me yesterday. I mean, I didn't score any goals, but I still played a good game.

It wasn't fair to them. I knew they wanted to be there, but work prevented it. I'd seen television cameras. Maybe there was a tape of the game my family could watch.

Percival and I went to the commissary for breakfast after the alarm went off. Neither of us talked very much. We both had too many nerves. At least Percival got to score a goal yesterday. I was still waiting for my chance to stand out.

We returned to the temporary dorms and put on our uniforms. When we walked through the arches and entered the stadium, we started talking.

"I can't believe I kicked that penalty right into the goal."

"I told you that you could do it. I'm just glad Daniel played like he was on a team."

"For a while! Why did he cream that guy from Jackson?"

We went on like that all the way to the locker room. The

coaches had set up cups of juice and two oatmeal raisin cookies on napkins. We sat down on the bench near our snacks while Coach Johnson spoke.

"You guys did a great job yesterday, but that was the easy part. Today, we're facing off with the best team in the region. Butterfield Academy."

"Since when are they the best?" Daniel griped.

"Since they won the other half of the brackets," Coach Stan growled. "Butterfield's coach has a great eye for talent. All of these guys are good enough to play anywhere in the world, and they're all on one team."

"You make it sound like we can't win," I said.

Coach Johnson gave me a look.

"Do you think we can't win?"

"No," I said. "I know we can win."

Coach Johnson smiled, his eyes shining.

"That's my boy."

His eyes narrowed.

"How's the face?"

"It's fine," I said. The truth was, my nose still kind of hurt, but I didn't want to wear the mask again. I'd already broken out in a heat rash on my forehead, where the straps were the tightest.

"Hmph. I've got my eye on you, Goalman. You'd better not be messing with me."

He gave me one last hard stare to make sure I got it. I did.

"All right, eat your snacks, and open those ears up.

We're going to hit you with some knowledge." Coach Johnson nodded to Coach Stan, who flipped the lights off.

Coach Bobby set up a projector to splash up onto the blank part of the locker room wall. The somewhat grainy footage was from the other bracket. I remembered taking notes about the Butterfield team when I'd been scouting between games.

"Precision, endurance, and skill," Coach Johnson said. "That's what our opponents bring to the table. They have the best fundamentals I've ever seen. Remember that the next time you guys want to whine about us drilling you too much. Drilling in practice leads to perfection on the field."

The Butterfield team continued to play on the screen. I watched them closely. A lot of the other guys on the team started to get bored. I could tell by the glazed-over look in their eyes.

They were being dumb. This wasn't just interesting. It was vital information.

"What do you guys notice about our opponents?" Coach Stan asked. "I want you guys thinking, not just sitting there, doing the inhale/exhale thing. It's time to shine."

No one else said anything, so I felt like I had to.

"The other team is always right where they need to be. They almost never miss a pass."

Coach Johnson pointed at me.

"Listen to Goalman, he has the right of it. Butterfield has no wasted motion. They don't waste time running up and down the pitch. They just get where they need to be in the first place."

On the screen, we watched while the Butterfield offensive

players expertly pinged the ball in a game of keep away. Their passing patterns made me dizzy. I lost sight of the ball until their striker, a big red-haired kid, smashed it into the goal.

Coach Johnson paused the screen on the red-haired kid.

"This is Seamus, the Butterfield striker. Don't let his size fool you, he's fast as a cheetah. Beware him, and don't let him get into position to score."

He started the video again. I took notes on their formations. Butterfield favored more defensive players than offensive, and focused on trying to keep possession of the ball. That was, until their lone two offensive players made opportunities to score.

"Butterfield is going to take the ball for most of the game," I blurted.

Coach Bobby's mean glare made me wilt in my seat.

"Way to be positive, Mr. Snoogie," Daniel said out of the corner of his mouth.

"I'm not trying to be disrespectful," I said quickly, looking at Coach Johnson. "But this is their strategy. This is their version of soccer. They're really good at keeping the ball, or at least keeping it away from their goal."

Coach Johnson and Coach Stan looked at each other and then at me.

"That's a good observation, Maxwell. What do you propose we do about it?"

Man, my mind decided to go on vacation and left its phone behind. I couldn't think of anything. My mouth opened, closed, and then I shook my head.

"I'm sorry, sir. I don't know."

"That's okay." Coach Johnson looked out over us to make it clear he spoke to the whole team and not just me. "Your three coaches haven't slept at all last night because we've been trying to come up with a counter to Butterfield's strategy. So this isn't an easy question, and it's not going to be an easy game."

Coach Stan changed the video display to an artist's rendering of a soccer field. I'd seen this type of software before. You can do all kinds of cool stuff, like experiment with different formations. They use a version of it on a couple of the video games I play.

"The standard defense to a 3-5-2 formation is 4-2-3-1."

The display changed, with the Cannons in red and Butterfield in blue rendered as blue dots. Rather than our names, the icons just listed positions.

"The idea of the 4-2-3-1 is to match numbers with numbers on the midfield, and take advantage of the wider areas. Now, a funny thing happens when — "

"Coach Stan, they're kids," Coach Johnson said.

Coach Stan looked sheepishly out at us.

"Sorry, guys. Now, where was I? Oh yes, Butterfield is ready for the standard response, but we don't really have much choice."

Coach Johnson looked right at me for a moment before he spoke.

"Our midfielders are going to work their butts off today, because you're going to have to play both ways. Offense and defense. Otherwise, we don't have a prayer of getting possession of the ball."

No wonder the coaches wanted us to show up early. I

usually like talking about soccer strategy, but it started to feel like school.

At least the cookies were good. It started to sink in, I mean finally sink in, just how much different playing for Caldwell felt compared to our games at the park. Pro soccer players attended meetings like this one with their coaches.

If I wanted to be the next Messi, I had to act like it. I sat up straight and dug out my pad to take notes. The coaches thought this was needed. Well, so did I, then.

A couple other guys on the team noticed my change in attitude. Daniel rolled his eyes and leaned back to nap. But Percival and Han got all studious, like me. It passed like a ripple through the team, so most of us were paying attention.

When the meeting wound up, the coaches surprised us with lunch from a local diner. The bag lunches included apple slices with caramel sauce, which is one of my most favorite things in the world even though I never really told anybody.

My stomach started doing flip-flops when we came out onto the pitch for the team introductions and handshakes. The arena was packed with people, there were news cameras, it felt almost like a real pro match rather than prep school athletics.

We lined up on the edge of the pitch while the La Forge president rambled on and on in a speech about the history of the tournament. I kept my eyes and attention focused on the other side of the field, where Butterfield's team faced off against us.

Their calm blew me away. Our team was a mess of nerves and eagerness and sheer panic. They stood like a bunch of statues. It looked to them as if they were about to go in for routine practice rather than a championship game.

"Max!"

I frowned at the sound of my name. The stadium was super loud, and sound did funny things. Sometimes I would think someone was talking to me, but it turned out to be my imagination.

"Max! Yeah, you, Max Goalman!"

Now I knew for sure I'd heard something. I whipped my head around until I spotted something I never expected to see: My sister, Emma, hanging halfway over the safety railing on the bleachers.

"Emma? What are you doing here?"

Coach Stan looked at me, looked at my sister, and then jutted his chin.

"You've got about five minutes. Go."

I shot him a grateful look and ran over to the bleachers.

"How did you get here? Do Mom and Dad know?"

She snorted.

"Are you dumb or something? Mom and Dad are here with me. You think I hitchhiked?"

It was a dumb question, now that I think about it. But I forgot all about feeling silly when Mom and Dad came down to join Emma at the rail.

"I thought you guys couldn't come."

"We rearranged things at the last minute," Mom said. "Besides, how could we miss your first championship game?"

"I heard from your friend Lobo that you got your face creamed in the first game of the tournament, and you had to wear a hideous mask for the last two days," Emma said.

"What?" Mom blurted, looking worried.

"First of all, Lobo is not my friend. She's a total brat and a bully. Second, I didn't get creamed. The doctor said I didn't break anything."

Emma acted like she didn't even hear me.

"Lobo says the mask is better looking than your real face, and you should wear it all the time. She told me to say that to you. And what else? Oh yeah. Good luck, Mr. Snoogie."

I glared at Dad.

"See what you did to me, Dad? Now, instead of having a cool nickname like Rex Rocket, everyone calls me Mr. Snoogie."

Mom shrugged.

"What's wrong with Mr. Snoogie?"

"What's not wrong with it?" I gasped.

"I think it's ironic," Mom said.

"What does that even mean?" I groaned.

"Goalman! Get back in line!"

Coach Stan's voice hit me like a lightning bolt. I stiffened up and then looked at my parents.

"I've got to go. Thanks for coming!"

CHAPTER 19

Moving Forward in Reverse

"There is no such thing as fun for the whole family."

— Jerry Seinfeld

"We'll be rooting for you, Max," Dad shouted.

"I'll make you proud!" I cried back.

"You already have," Mom said, but then I had to run out onto the pitch with the rest of the team. We walked by and shook the hands of our opponents, one by one. Even then, Butterfield acted like robots. They barely even breathed.

"I think these guys are all androids," Han said.

"Or aliens," Alex added. "Are you ready to run your legs off, Mr. Snoogie?"

I growled, using the anger at my nickname to fuel me.

"I'm so ready! After watching all of that footage, we should know what Butterfield is going to do before they do."

"Mr. Snoogie is right," Daniel said. "We've got this."

"Yeah, but..." Alex stared at the line of statues facing off against us. "Isn't the way they're acting kind of, um, scary?"

"That just means they don't want it as bad as we do," I said.

The crowd grew quiet as they prepared for the coin toss. Coach Johnson chose heads. The coin spun in the air, flashing bright in the sunlight. The ref slapped it onto the back of his hand.

"Tails."

Butterfield's coach chose to take the kickoff. We got into position on our half of the pitch. Daniel and I were ready to help the midfield and potentially move into scoring position. We knew they would come and try to take the ball, then keep it away from us. Alex was our striker, the only player dedicated solely to offense.

But a funny thing happened after the kickoff. As Percival collected the ball and started dribbling up the pitch, Butterfield's players surged forward. All of a sudden, they didn't look like robots. Their eyes burned with the same intensity I saw in the mirror every day before a match.

Butterfield didn't want it less than us. They wanted it just as bad. This was going to be a grueling, grueling game.

Butterfield made a blistering start. Despite having our midfielders backing up our defensive line, Butterfield's left-winger took possession of the ball.

I raced along the outside edge of a mob of players, all

scrambling. Our side wanted to tackle. Their side wanted to stop us.

I saw an opening and darted inside. Keeping my body over the ball, I went for a side tackle but the striker duped me. He used fancy footwork to transfer the ball behind him, where the Butterfield striker had been lurking out of sight.

Their striker tore past our defenders, dribbling for our goal. Vince stood ready, legs spread out in a half-crouch. At least the striker wouldn't take our goaltender off guard.

Butterfield's striker broke into the left, leaving Percival behind. He now had an unguarded shot on our goaltender. The striker faked to the left and then rocketed the ball with a kick to the right corner of our goal.

Vince almost fell over changing direction. He jumped, body going horizontal as he sought to block the shot. The ball smacked into his gloved hand and bounced away.

No one was close enough to collect the ball. It rolled out of bounds, and a ref blew his whistle. Butterfield now had the chance for a throw-in, deep on our half of the pitch.

We lined up for the throw-in. I couldn't believe how well they'd penetrated our defenses. Even with us matching them in numbers. Butterfield knew how to play their version of soccer.

The Butterfield midfielder tossed the ball into play. I wound up in a duel for possession against the Butterfield winger. Our movement slowed to a crawl as we struggled against each other.

He got the better of me by kicking the ball unexpectedly toward his half of the pitch. The Butterfield attacking midfielder collected the ball and dribbled laterally to the right half of the pitch. Just when Percival and Han were about to tackle it away from him, he passed to the striker.

Their striker took his shot immediately, hoping to take Vince by surprise. I didn't have time to check if our goaltender was ready. I jumped in front of the shot, keeping my arms out to my sides, and took it right in the chest.

The ball ricocheted off the bottom of my chin. It made my nose hurt, even though that's not where I took the shot. I stumbled when I fell and went down.

Our fullbacks collected the ball, but Butterfield's midfield defensive line swarmed them. I tried to get up in time to cover their striker, but I was too late. He took another shot at our goal. Vince caught it out of the air, and I could have fainted with relief.

Now Vince had the ball. He faked like he was about to throw the ball back into play, then kicked it hard toward their half of the pitch.

We all ran like a pack of wolves was on our heels. Daniel sprinted out ahead of the pack, putting his long legs to use.

I went to back him up, but the Butterfield midfielder cut me off. I tried to get around him, but he matched my every move. It was as if they'd watched video of us...

It hit me then that they probably had. They were just as prepared as us and more experienced at these big events.

That meant we just had to work harder. I pushed myself, making my tired legs move faster than ever. I overtook their midfielder and put myself into position to take a pass.

Alex, smothered by two fullbacks, heel-kicked the ball my way. I claimed the ball and dribbled toward the right side of their goal.

Their goaltender watched me with laser focus. I kicked

the ball toward the bottom left of the goal. He drove for it, flopping hard on his chest as his fingers closed just behind the ball.

The ball hit the net, and I skidded to a halt in the grass. I stared at the ball, rolling away from the net after the goal, because I couldn't believe it. I had actually scored.

"Mr. Snoogie!" Daniel slapped me on the back so hard I almost fell over. "You did it!"

I looked over at the stands. I couldn't make my family out among the crowd; it was just too far away, but I knew they were there.

An energy passed through me, and my legs just weren't tired any longer. I ran back to our half of the pitch while Coach Johnson applauded.

"Nice shot, Goalman."

They kicked the ball onto our half of the pitch. Alex scooped it up and dribbled, flanked by Daniel and me. Their mob of defensive players charged our line. We spread out further from each other, and Alex passed the ball to me.

I raced to the right, knowing I had no hope of getting much deeper onto their half. But I just needed to keep possession long enough for our defensive line to catch up.

Their midfielder darted up on my right and slide tackled the ball away from me. My heart hammered faster than ever as I ran after it, but by then their winger had taken charge. Their passing game confused me, leaving me chasing my own tail.

I turned with the tide and ran back toward our goal. Our defensive line bunched up, slowing the progress. Things got so crazy it was hard to make out what happened, but I managed to keep my eye on the ball.

During a furious duel, the ball shot up almost straight into the air. I jogged backward, gauging where it would come down, and lined myself up to take possession. Unfortunately, the attacking midfielder from Butterfield had the same idea.

Our knees collided painfully, causing us to stagger. I recovered just a little quicker and dribbled the ball back toward their goal.

I could hear the other team galloping behind me. Any time we managed to get possession, it was like Butterfield went into overdrive until they got it back. I fended off an attempt to tackle from both sides at once.

The two defenders moved in like pinchers, trying to cut me off and slow me down. I spotted Daniel out of the corner of my eye. I passed the ball his way, but the Butterfield striker stepped in and stole the ball.

I ground to a halt and ran back the other way, struggling to catch back up to the ball. I watched as the Butterfield striker went down in a tangle of arms and legs. The ball bounced out of bounds, and our side got the throw-in since Butterfield made contact last.

The throw-in gave us a potential edge, but we were deep back on our half of the field. Vince stood with his hands on his knees, a resting position that he could move quickly from. He fully expected Butterfield to get possession and try for a goal.

I couldn't say he would be wrong. Even after watching their previous games, it was nearly impossible to keep the ball away from Butterfield. They always seemed to be in the right place at the right time, except for my goal earlier.

As we lined up for the throw-in, I tried to think of a way to create a situation like that again. Han faked a toss toward their end of the pitch and then put the ball right in front of me. I immediately dribbled forward as Percival and our winger moved to block for me.

With their help, I evaded the Butterfield defensive line and broke through. Nothing but a long expanse of green grass separated me from the goal. My heat pounded in my chest, and not just because I ran full out. Somehow, we'd managed to penetrate the unbreakable wall of their defense.

I remembered my training with Paul. It wasn't just about how fast you could dribble. It was about creating a situation where I couldn't help but score.

That morning, we'd watched tons of footage on Butterfield. Their goaltender was phenomenal, but he had a weakness. He thought too much. His reactions were much better when he didn't have time to think.

I checked over my shoulder with a quick glance. I still had about fifteen feet of space between me and the closest defender. I angled myself toward the left side, knowing it would let the pack catch up soon.

I slowed way down when I was only five feet from the goal but all the way near the corner. Their goaltender's eyes bored into me. They practically screamed that I wouldn't get it past him.

The defenders were almost on top of me. I had to take the shot. I hooked the ball with my toes and lifted it, making sure it moved up as well as away from me.

The goaltender's hands were about six inches too low to catch the ball. It smacked him on the inner elbows and then rolled up and hit him right in the kisser.

He flinched and sent the ball careening into the net. The goaltender snatched the ball up. Man, if looks could kill, I would have been a goner. I'd never seen so much hatred in someone's eyes before.

"Way to go, Goalman," Han said, jogging up beside me. "It's about time you started letting loose."

The Butterfield coach requested a time-out, and he got it. We went back to the benches and hydrated. Coach Johnson came up and knelt before me.

"How are you doing, Max? You good?"

"I'm fine," I said between pants.

"You've been running like a maniac and it's unseasonably hot. Are you sure you're okay?"

"I'll be alright."

He nodded.

"I'll keep my eye on you. I might pull you out and give you a rest."

I gasped.

"I don't need a rest, Coach."

He shook his head.

"You might think differently. Butterfield just put in Seamus and their other star players."

We went back to the pitch when time-out ended. Across the field from us, Seamus stood out because of his height as much as his shock of red hair. He kicked off, shooting the ball toward us like a meteor.

CHAPTER 20
Spazzing Out

*"If I wasn't a golfer, I would still be miserable —
but not as miserable."*

— Larry David

It landed deep on our half, so deep it was Percival who collected it. He moved it up the field and then passed to Han. Daniel and I moved to flank Han and keep the Butterfield defenders away.

We crossed the middle line when Seamus zipped up on our right side. I knew he was coming to tackle. I tried to block him, but he faked me out and darted behind me.

He tried to tackle the ball from Han, but Han managed to juke him. But Han slowed down enough that the rest of the defenders caught up with our little three-man offensive.

Things got ugly. Some jerk snuck in a good kick to my thigh when we all bunched up over the ball. I cried out, grabbing my leg as a cramp ran its way through the muscle. I stumbled and nearly fell.

By the time I got moving again, Butterfield had moved the ball all the way back to our end of the pitch. I didn't know who kicked me, but I felt like it might have been Seamus. I pointedly looked at the ref as I ran past, but he didn't seem to notice.

I slowed to a jog as I came up on a grand melee of scrambling players. The ball passed from them, to us, and back again. I couldn't get close enough to make a difference.

Seamus swept in and snatched possession of the ball. I tried to get around the mob to reach him, but I knew it was too late.

He lashed a low shot across the goal, just barely missing the post. It streaked past Vince at a tight angle and hit the net. Seamus clenched his fists and bellowed like an angry giant. The crowd went nuts. The score now stood at 2 to 1.

Coach Johnson blew his whistle.

"Goalman, bench!"

My heart sank as I jogged back to the bench as another player took my place on the field. I stopped off and got a cup of cold sports drink before sitting down. As much as I hated to be benched, I knew Coach Johnson was right. I needed some time to recover.

That didn't mean it was easy to sit there and watch my team struggle. Seamus was a phenom, and not just offensively. He bounced back and forth between his twin roles like a champion.

Plus, he was fresh. Even after Coach Johnson pulled a few more of our guys, including Daniel and Alex, and replaced them with new players, Seamus left them in the dust.

"Does this guy ever get tired?" Coach Stan muttered as Seamus dribbled past our position.

"He has to get tired," I said.

Coach Johnson switched up our formation, weighting us toward offense. The results weren't great. With our midfielders outnumbered by Butterfield, we couldn't keep possession of the ball to save our souls.

I wound up standing in front of the bench and shouting out encouragement to our team. It was the best I could do. I really hoped to be put back in soon. I'd hate to think my parents arrived just to watch me play the first quarter of a game.

About a minute before halftime, it looked like our team was about to score. But Seamus won the ball back on the edge of his own goal. He took off like his pants were on fire, getting all the way in scoring distance of our goal in about fifteen seconds.

He took his shot. Vince made the jump but came up short. I groaned and covered my face with my hands as we hit halftime. Butterfield had just evened up the score.

Since it was the championship game, we had to sit through a long performance by the La Forge marching band. It gave us the time to regroup and strategize, though.

"We're getting murdered out there," Coach Johnson said, smacking his tablet. "You have got to cover their attacks better."

"Seamus is too fast, Coach," Daniel said.

"Too fast? Is he a Cheetah? Or a race car?" Coach Johnson demanded.

"Well, no — "

"Then he's not too fast! If you can't handle him alone, double up on him. Triple up on him."

I shot my hand up into the air. I almost threw up when Coach Johnson actually called on me.

"Yes, what is it, Goalman?"

"I'm sorry, but I don't think doubling up on Seamus will work."

Coach Bobby snorted like a pig.

"What makes you think you know better than us, Goalman?"

I swallowed the lump in my throat. It turned into a brick in my stomach, but I had to keep going. I'd already brought it up.

"It's not that I think I know better. I just noticed that other teams have tried to double up on Seamus and it hasn't worked. If they double up on him, he just switches to more defense."

"Then what do you want us to do? Just ignore him?" Daniel asked.

"No, of course not. I think we should try and wear him out. Work heavy offense and keep him chasing the ball back and forth across the pitch."

Halftime ended. I was so happy when Coach Johnson put me back in as attacking midfielder. The grass felt right under my cleats. Sunlight warmed the pitch up, creating a smell of grass that mingled with the Gatorade I'd spilled on my shirt. I like to think of that as a uniquely soccer smell.

I stopped to fix my shin guard, then got into a ready position as we prepared for the kickoff. The score was even. It was still anybody's game, with half the time remaining.

The ball bounced onto Butterfield's half of the field.

Seamus scooped it up and came dribbling in hard.

Daniel, Alex, and I ran up on Seamus, but not to block him. Daniel tried a tackle, but Seamus spun around in a tight circle and juked it. Alex came in for his own attempt, but it was just a trick. Seamus took the bait and veered away from Alex.

That left him ripe pickings for a slide tackle. I timed it just right, thumping the ball over to Daniel. He only had a lonely fullback on him as he dribbled hard for the enemy goal.

We bunched up about twenty feet from the Butterfield goal. I tried to work my way inside, so I could back up Alex and Daniel. The Butterfield defenders formed a living wall that made my attempt impossible.

At last, I saw an opening and broke through. I tackled the ball away from the Butterfield winger. I had nowhere to go but toward the white line marking out of bounds.

Seamus and his striker came in fast. I couldn't take a shot at the goal, and I had no easy passes close by.

I had to take a risk. I shot the ball up high, sending it up and over the heads of Seamus and his striker. Our center took possession, dribbling the ball almost the second it landed.

I had my head turned, watching the ball. That was probably what saved me when Seamus ran me over like a freight train. His chest smacked into the side of my head, and the next thing I knew, I was rolling in the grass.

At least he hadn't hit my fragile nose. As it was, a light trickle of blood warmed my nostrils when I finally came to a stop and struggled to my feet.

"That jerk," Alex said, helping me up the last few inches.

"What happened?"

"He tried to run you over. He did it on purpose. At least the ref is calling it this time."

Seamus got a yellow card. The crowd made a lot of noise. About half of them seemed to be mad that Seamus was being penalized, showing how partisan the crowd really was.

All I knew was, my parents had seen me get steamrolled by a much bigger kid. I hoped that wouldn't start another round of "soccer's too dangerous" from them.

I sniffled the blood back up and wiped my face. Fortunately, it stopped bleeding pretty quick. By the time I stepped out for my penalty kick, I was breaking normally again, without the wet sniffling sound.

Their goaltender looked downright scary. I knew he would hate it if I managed to score on him yet again, even on a penalty kick. Well, I didn't care if he hated it. Seamus shouldn't have knocked me over.

I tried not to look at Seamus, but I couldn't help it. He had this look on his face like he was totally laid back and relaxed. As if he hadn't done anything wrong at all and didn't care that his behavior was giving us a free shot at their goal.

I turned my attention back to the goaltender. I knew he could snatch balls up if they came in low or medium height. He did have a weakness when it came to higher shots, even if they came in direct.

If I wanted to score on him while he was totally ready for it, I would have to take advantage of his weakness. When it came to scoring, I preferred to attack low. I had trouble gauging the right height otherwise, and my shots would go over the net rather than in it, or bounce off the guardrail.

But it was really the only chance I had. I hadn't trained

on shooting goals as much as I'd have liked to with Paul. We focused on fundamentals, things I'd missed out on because I hadn't had private soccer tutors growing up.

Now, I really wished we'd spent at least one morning or afternoon covering penalty kicks. Statistically, most penalty kicks resulted in no goal. But that didn't mean I could just give up. I could imagine my family's eyes on me, watching my every move.

I couldn't let my sister see me give up, or my parents. I took a long, deep breath and let it out slowly, then ran up on the ball. I smashed the ball, sending it on an upward angle.

Their goaltender was caught off guard. He raced along under the net, trying to catch the ball in time. He wasn't going to make it. I could see it.

But my shot bounced off the metal and shot back out onto the pitch. I'd aimed a little bit too high. The team tried to be nice about it, but I felt miserable, like I'd failed them all.

After the penalty, we tried to rally. With a combination of luck and trickery, we managed to get past their fullbacks and corner and close in on the goal. Alex sent a shot right into their goaltender's gloves. He stood up as both teams bunched up around the enemy net.

The goaltender looked toward Seamus. I crab walked over to block him, but that left their midfielder unguarded. I was torn about what to do and eventually went to block the midfielder. Seamus was faster than me. I probably couldn't stop him from getting possession.

I had a better shot at the midfielder. We were closer in speed and size. Fortunately, Daniel came around and guarded Seamus. Those two were evenly matched.

I guess the Butterfield goaltender thought the same thing

because he tossed the ball to the Butterfield winger. The winger dribbled immediately for our half of the pitch. I ran after, angling myself across the field so I could get into position for a counterattack.

I predicted that their winger would get a shot off before we could close in on him, but I also predicted that Vince would stop him cold. The winger wasn't that great at scoring, not that he had to be with Seamus and his pet striker around.

The winger took his shot. Vince pounced on the ball, hugging it to his chest and tumbling into a somersault. I cringed, fearing he would drop the ball.

He came back up to his feet and instantly tossed it in my direction. I almost got caught off guard. Just in time, I hooked the ball out of the air with my toes and dribbled back toward their goal.

Because I'd put myself out wide in their right, near the corner, I had no Butterfield players blocking me. They all galloped like wild horses, trying to catch up, but I ran down the right side of the pitch.

The boundary line got closer and closer as Seamus and his striker hemmed me in. Worse, a Butterfield fullback came right at me, cutting me off in three directions.

I had to divert to my left. This let Seamus catch up and go for a tackle. His cleats collided with the back of my calf, sending my leg out wide. We both went down, skimming along the grass. The fullback tried to take possession but only succeeded in bouncing it out of bounds.

The whistle blared. I thought it was for Seamus' foul, but they didn't see it or they thought it was an accident. Judging by the dirty look Seamus gave me, it wasn't an accident. He wanted to hurt me.

But the out-of-bounds call gave us a chance to get back

at Seamus by scoring another goal. Alex threw the ball in to Daniel, who took off like a rocket ship.

A lot of quick breaks followed. Butterfield tackled the ball away, but we took it back before they reached our half of the pitch. Almost the entirety of both teams wound up battling it out right near the middle of the field.

The ball got lost in the tumult. I finally saw it right before Percival stumbled and flopped on top. A Butterfield player tripped over Percival, and then one of our guys tripped over him, and pretty soon, the refs were blasting whistles because half the players were on the ground.

They decided there was no way to determine who had possession last, and we went back to a coin flip for a new kickoff. The coaches were crabbing that it wasn't normal practice, and that we should have had possession, but there was nothing they could do about it.

CHAPTER 21
Repo Kids

"Procrastinate now, don't put it off."

— Johnny Carson

A kick off seemed fair enough to me. We won the coin toss, but the coaches chose to receive. I guess they really wanted to get the ball back.

The kick came in deep in our half. We crossed over fast as lightning, but Butterfield was there to meet us. Our corner touched the ball just enough to steer it to me. I watched it come in, spinning in the opposite direction it traveled. Bits of grass flew up in the air and caught the bright sunlight.

It all seemed to happen in slow motion. I gathered the ball up and bounced it between my feet, juking the Butterfield defender who tried to tackle me. Dribbling toward their goal, I kept aware of everything going on around me.

Everything just kind of clicked. I reached the point of soccer nirvana that only guys like Messi are supposed to achieve. I didn't feel panicked about Seamus running up on me, or angry that he'd fouled me twice.

That didn't mean I felt nothing. I had this urge, this drive to get the ball in the net. I wanted it more than anything, but I also knew how to do it.

I slowed myself to a near halt and let Seamus run past me. With a quick heel pass, I sent the ball to Alex and then jogged along the outside of the Butterfield defensive line. Alex switch-kicked the ball to Han, who passed it over to me.

I was still a long way off from the goal. The smart thing would have been to pass the ball again to keep possession of it.

But our play was to wear Seamus out. I knew the only way to do that was to make him chase me. I dribbled like I was going to run the ball right into their net.

The move hooked Seamus like a trout. He ran up behind me, pushing himself to the max. He might have been faster than me, but he was also bigger. He had to move an extra twenty, thirty pounds up and down the pitch compared to me, every single time.

His cleats tore up the grass, closing the distance between us. I pushed it even further, the championship spurring me on. My parents were there. I wanted them to see me at my absolute best.

Seamus slowly, painfully, started to fall behind me. He made an angry sound and caught up again. I took my shot, which their goaltender deflected back out into play.

But I'd done what I wanted. Seamus was too gassed out to take possession of the ball. I got hold of it first and sent a hooking pass over to Alex.

Alex got swarmed by their fullback and corner, and lost

the ball. The game moved back to our half of the pitch before our fullbacks ground the progress to a halt.

Seamus caught up at last and tried to tackle. He managed to get the better of Han, sending the smaller boy down as he took the ball away.

But Seamus' pass was a little bit too slow. Daniel zipped up between Seamus and his striker and stole the ball, dribbling toward their goal again.

Daniel came in on the left, then slowed down. He checked to see the Butterfield defenders coming in on him. Instead of taking his shot, he dribbled a little bit further to the left.

"Shoot!" I cried, but he couldn't hear me over the crowd.

Daniel waited just a little bit too long. Just as he was about to kick, the Butterfield fullback snatched possession of the ball and sent it back down the field. The Butterfield striker caught it up, and alarms went off in my head.

As long as the striker had the ball, we were in trouble. Vince was a decent goaltender, but he struggled against tricky strikers. And believe me, that Butterfield striker was so tricky he should have been a magician.

I took off after the striker. Seamus tried to keep up with me, but he hadn't recovered yet. The striker had to cross almost the entire pitch to reach our goal.

The striker knew his tank had gotten pretty low. He slowed his pace and started looking for someone he could pass to.

Things got really crazy. It was like all the players on both teams gathered in the same ten-yard space, me included. I kept my eye on the ball, even when someone kicked me in the back of my calf. I think it was an accident, though. Everyone just wanted to get possession of the ball, and I got caught in the crossfire.

I ignored the pain and kept after the ball. Percival and their corner both went for a tackle and crashed together right in front of me. Percival's face actually moved; that's how hard they hit each other.

They went down in a heap. I jumped over them and landed about three feet from the unattended ball.

Seamus and I came in on opposite sides of the ball. I kept my body over the ball, I held my balance, and he still got the better of me. I stumbled, tripping over the ball and Seamus' feet. Seamus also went down, but that slick dude snapped his leg out and made an aerial pass to their striker.

The striker came in like a hurricane. He lined himself up right in front of Vince. Normally, doing that is a really dumb idea unless you take the goaltender by surprise. You're essentially just passing possession of the ball.

But Vince was scared. Their striker had worked his way into our goaltender's head. The striker went for a low kick to the corner of the goal. Vince darted to the side to intercept.

Only, the striker faked us out. He switched to his left leg and smacked the ball so hard I felt it in my stomach. The ball zipped right over Vince's head and hit the net.

It was one of the most beautiful things I'd ever seen. They had just taken the lead, I should have been really upset. I mean, I was worried. But at the same time, I really appreciated the striker's technique and skill.

"Nice shot man," I said as I passed the striker on his way to the other side of the field.

His smile faded for a moment, and then he looked me in the eye.

"What did you just say to me, Kid?"

"I said, nice shot."

He blinked.

"Why would you tell me that?"

"Because it was a good play. It won't work twice, though. That's the last goal your team scores this game."

He chuckled and jogged backward, spreading his hands out.

"We'll just see about that, Mr. Snoogie."

I groaned. How did everyone keep learning that name?

Alex jogged up to me while both teams set themselves on their half of the pitch.

"What did you say to that thick-neck?"

"I told that thick-neck he made a nice shot. I was trying to be, um, sportsmanlike."

"Oh. Well, they have the lead, Max. How can we possibly win?"

"We just have to score two more times, and we win."

"As long as they don't score on us again. That striker has Vince's number. All I'm saying."

We prepared to receive the kickoff. I was super glad Paul had trained me so hard before the tournament. Every other player's uniform had changed color because it had soaked through with sweat. I definitely had dark puts, but overall, I was in better shape than anyone else on the field.

I looked at the clock. Less than a quarter time remaining. That wasn't much time to make two goals.

Alex was worried. I could tell Coach Johnson was worried, too. He held his tablet in a death grip while making notes on it.

I hoped he had a great strategy to pull out because Alex was right to be worried. If I were watching this game on the outside, I would pretty much bet that Butterfield was going to win.

But I wasn't watching the game. I wasn't even playing a video game version of it. I was playing in a championship tournament.

My dad loves to watch really old movies, like the one with the boxer who talks funny. He used to say, "It ain't over until it's over," along with the guy in the movie.

"It ain't over until it's over," I said, even though nobody else could hear me. The ball whiffed through the air, spinning so fast the black and white turned gray.

The ball came in at a high angle. It could wind up almost all the way to our goal. I knew it would hurt, but I jumped in the air and turned my face to the side.

I caught the ball right on the highest part of my chest. It hit my throat a little bit, too, though. I landed on my feet, but I spent a few seconds coughing.

Han was there, though, in the nick of time to sweep up the ball. He fended off a tackle attempt, spinning around and catching the ball with his trailing foot to keep it moving forward. I recovered enough to start running, feeling at my neck.

I was pretty sure I had the ball logo tattooed on my throat at that point. It didn't hurt as bad as getting my nose busted, but it didn't feel good, either.

Han was on a tear. He ripped through their defenders and broke free of the pack, streaking toward the Butterfield goal.

214

But the Butterfield fullbacks were all over him. They positioned themselves in a pincer move, coming in on him from both sides.

Daniel was in a great position. Unmarked, no one was anywhere near him. He waited for the pass, and I was sure Han would see it, too.

But Han had this look in his eyes like he wanted to be the hero. He shot almost straight at the Butterfield keeper. Daniel's mouth fell open in shock. We very well could have scored.

I held my breath as the ball sped toward the net. The goaltender took two steps to the side and snatched the ball out of the air without seeming to try.

"Darn it, Han!" I growled. "Why didn't you pass?"

Daniel slapped me on the back pretty hard.

"Be positive, Mr. Snoogie. You know how it is when the blood gets pumping and you want to murder that ball right into the net. He got carried away."

I stopped and stared at Daniel. He was right. I should have been more understanding of my team.

The goaltender set up like he was going to kick the ball deep onto our half of the field. We all moved back some, but I worried he might be faking us out.

Sure enough, the goaltender threw the ball to their corner instead of taking the kick. The corner shot like a streak of lighting on the left side of the pitch, about a yard from the boundary line.

Our defense moved to compensate, blocking his path and snuffing out the danger. The corner shot a low pass to Seamus, who took up the dribbling without missing a step.

I came up on his left side, stretching my legs out to the

max. If he hadn't been gassed out, I would never have caught up. I came in with a slide tackle and shot the ball away from him.

Seamus did something you can never do on the pitch. He panicked. His hand shot out and slapped the ball before I could complete my pass to Daniel.

The refs blew the whistle. Interference would probably give us a throw-in, I remember thinking. I mean, that's what would have happened if Seamus hadn't really lost.

He grabbed the ball in both his hands and stood over me. His face turned bright red and then he threw the ball at my face full-force. I got my arm up in front of my face just in time, but the impact made me conk myself in the forehead with my wrist.

I couldn't figure out which hurt worse, my wrist or my already-sore nose. More whistles followed. Seamus should have been red-carded. That didn't happen, though. They called for a penalty kick, but the refs didn't even seem to care that was Seamus' second foul of the game.

I didn't see any point in worrying about it, though. His dumb move had earned me a penalty kick. If I scored, I would tie up the game.

We couldn't set up for the penalty kick, though. Coach Bobby stormed onto the field and got right in the head ref's face.

CHAPTER 22
Strange Allies

"A day without sunshine is like, you know, night."

— Steve Martin

"**A**re you blind? Do you need glasses? Why did you not red card that mean little brat?"

"Sir, get off the pitch," the ref said.

"I'll get off the pitch when you card that blatant foul! He should be out of the game."

"Your team has a penalty kick. It's a championship game."

"Oh, so the rules don't matter because it's a championship game?"

Coach Bobby, of all people, standing up for me was pretty weird. I had thought he had it in for me from the start. My mom says that sometimes people surprise you in moments of crisis. I guess this was one of those situations.

The ref tried to move past Coach Bobby and set up the penalty kick, but Coach Bobby grabbed his arm.

The ref blew his whistle and pointed at the stadium exit.

"That's it, you're out of here, Pal."

"What?"

Coach Bobby sure was mad. I thought his head would explode. If Coach Johnson and Coach Stan hadn't come out and pushed Bobby toward the exit, there might have been a fight.

As messed up as that was, I now had to prepare to take a penalty kick. My wrist was red and hot and swollen. I didn't think it was broken, but it would be sore for a while. At least I didn't run on my hands. I wouldn't let it slow me down.

My face hurt, too. I could feel blood trying to trickle out my nose, but I kept sucking it back up. I didn't want anyone to see, and get pulled from the game.

I faced off against the Butterfield goaltender. He stood in a half-crouch, ready to move in any direction. I guess he respected me, because he didn't act all cocky or smile. He was taking me dead serious.

The ref tossed me the ball. I caught it on my toe, bounced it around a little bit, and then planted it on the grass in front of me. I rested my left foot on top of the ball to steady it and stared across the grass at the goal.

What would Messi do? He liked to take power shots at the corner, but not every time. Messi would get in the goaltender's head; that's what he would do. Could I do the same thing?

I set myself mentally as if I was one hundred percent guaranteed to make the goal. I knew I couldn't pretend.

I had to believe it. Butterfield hadn't switched out their keeper for the entire game. He had to be tired.

Power was the way to go. I jogged back a little bit. Then I ran up to the ball as the crowd fell almost silent.

I smashed the ball toward the corner. For a second I thought it might go too high and hit the rail. The keeper jumped, hands straining to reach the ball.

The ball sank perfectly into the net, inches from the keeper's fingers and the barest eyelash from hitting the rim. The crowd exploded. A bunch of guys, including Alex and Han, came up and patted me on the back and mussed my hair.

"Way to go, Goalman. You tied us up." Alex grinned. "I should have listened to you."

"It ain't over until it's over," I said, trying to sound cool. Percival took the wrong idea, though. Or maybe the right one.

"Maxwell is most astute," he said, his face bright red and a sheen of sweat covering him head to toe. "We still must score one more goal to win, and there's not much time left on the clock."

"Will they give us overtime?" I asked.

Alex shrugged.

"I don't know, but they probably should."

I gathered them up into a huddle.

"Look, guys, I think the refs might want Butterfield to win. Let's not leave it up to them giving us overtime. Let's make sure there's no doubt who the better team is."

"It's us!" Daniel growled, thrusting his fist in the air.

"You bet it is. Seamus is gassed out, and their striker isn't much better. Think you can handle them, Percival?"

"I'll do my best."

I looked at Daniel, Alex, and Han.

"The four of us need to work together. Let's win this game, win this tournament, and then drown ourselves in pizza and Gatorade."

"Now you're speaking my language," Han said with a wink. "And don't worry, I'll look for the pass before I try taking another shot by myself. That was dumb."

I looked over at Daniel before I replied.

"It's all right, Han. We've all been there."

We tried our strategy, matching offense with offense. Alex and Han loped along the right side of the field, keeping pace with Daniel and I.

Seamus and his striker barreled toward us like a pair of bulls. I swear, I could see steam coming out of Seamus' nostrils.

"Pass!" Daniel hollered. He knew what I did, that Seamus wanted to cream me.

I didn't pass, though. I kept right on toward Seamus. He moved slightly to the left, preparing himself for a simple tackle. Not a bad strategy, but I faked him out. I switched feet and then dropped to the grass, slide-kicking a pass to Daniel.

Seamus tripped over my leg and flopped onto the grass face-first. I squirmed to my feet and tried to catch up to the ball. Daniel dribbled to within ten feet of their goal, totally unmarked by defenders.

Daniel glanced around, but he could see that no one else

was in a good position to take his pass. He took a shot at the goal instead, pounding the ball in a low shot toward the left corner.

The keeper went sideways, putting his hands together to intercept the ball. He flopped hard on his side, his face all twisted up in pain, but the ball bounced off his hands instead of hitting the net.

The rebound ball was still in play. Han snapped up possession but he couldn't hang onto it while two fullbacks smothered him with tackle attempts.

Han tried a pass to Alex, but the Butterfield striker scooped it up and ran for our goal. Almost half a dozen players swarmed up to either tackle or block for the strike. I avoided a dirty elbow from Seamus and managed to toe kick the ball away from their striker.

Unfortunately, no one else touched it before the ball went out of bounds. The refs blew the whistle, and the striker got to do a throw-in from the border.

I felt dumb for not checking how close we were to the boundary before going after a tackle. I got too focused on getting the ball away from the striker. I guess I didn't have faith in Vince, and it had cost me. Maybe even cost us the game if Butterfield took full advantage of the throw-in.

"Don't sweat it, Maxwell," Percival said while we lined up for the throw-in. "You stopped their momentum, at the least."

"As long as they don't get it right back," I mumbled. I looked up at the stands, using my hand to shield my eyes from the sun.

We were close enough to the north side of the stadium where my family was seated. I strained my eyes until I made them out. My mom stood there with her hands clasped in front of her, looking real worried. I could only see the top of Emma's head, but my dad stood behind her, slurping on a soda.

He noticed me looking at him.

"Go Max!" Dad shouted, which would have been real supportive but he belched at the end of it.

Because the crowd had fallen quiet while the refs set up the throw-in, that belch carried like a mountain yodel. A lot of people laughed. I wanted to sink into the earth and disappear.

The throw-in flew over onto their side of the field. The Butterfield winger raced after the ball and swept his foot around to hook it into a pass.

Daniel tried to intercept the pass but he didn't quite make it. The ball skidded across the grass while a half dozen players gave chase. Seamus caught the pass but immediately had to fend off tackle attempts from our team.

Seamus dragged the ball behind him and thumped it on his heel. It took me a second to realize he was going for a Rainbow.

His placement didn't go quite right, though. The ball came down almost on top of his head instead of landing in front of him. Seamus struggled, then tripped over the ball and tumbled through the grass.

Han swept the ball and ran for the goal. I paced beside him, in case he needed to pass or a block. Sure enough, the Butterfield striker came in hot from the left side.

I moved to keep myself between him and Han. The striker crowded me, trying to intimidate me into making a mistake. But I knew he wouldn't take the risk of giving us another penalty kick. Not with so little time left on the clock.

I kept my cool and continued to block his access to Han. But all of a sudden, Han went down hard in the grass. I jogged to a halt and looked back to see what happened. It looked like Seamus had gone for a slide tackle and wound up tripping both himself and Han.

The ball bounced away, free and clear for whoever could claim it. I made my move, running up on the ball and dribbling it back toward their goal. Five of their players swooped up on me at once.

I looked for a pass, but there was no way to get one through. I'd be just giving the ball back to the other team. But I had an idea. If I had to put the ball back in Butterfield's hands, I would at least take a shot at their goal.

I was almost thirty feet out, but I rocketed a shot at their goal. The Butterfield goaltender hadn't been paying attention. He scrambled like crazy to block my shot, tackling the ball and falling onto the ground inside the goal.

He got up holding the ball like a dragon hoarding its treasure. At that point, I was joined by four of my teammates, evening the odds with their defensive players. Yes, I'd given possession of the ball back to the other team.

But now their goalkeeper had a choice. Try and throw-in and hope his team got possession, or kick it as far onto our half of the pitch as possible. If he did the kick though, we'd have possession of the ball again.

I tried to psych out the keeper. I stared right at him as I moved back and forth and side to side. The Cannons all stayed in motion, while Butterfield looked pretty gassed out.

I think I might have freaked out the keeper a little,

because he went for the kick. Even if he were giving possession back to us, he kept it away from our offensive line, including me.

The kick was pretty solid because Percival picked it up about ten feet from our goal. He dribbled forward, unmarked and clear for the moment.

I knew it wouldn't last. I caught Daniel and Alex's attention, then pointed at the enemy goal.

"Stay put, I'm going to get it to you," I cried as I took off after the mob of kids charging the ball.

The sun beat down on my head like nobody's business. I swear every individual hair on my head had been filled up with boiling hot sunlight. The air I heaved into my lungs felt swampy and tasted like grass.

No doubt about it. This game was the most intense I'd ever played. As hard as the game had been, I realized that I'd never been happier in my entire life.

I felt alive, like really alive. Sweat poured off my body, and my throat was raw from so much breathing, but I was having the time of my life. This was where I belonged. I finally accepted that the soccer field would always be my real home.

After I realized that, well, it was just plain easier to ignore all the discomfort. My mom once told me that every moment of pleasure in life has to be purchased with effort or pain. I was putting in plenty of effort and pain in this tournament, and this game especially.

I accepted the sore legs, and the aching nose, and the intense heat because all I could care about was that moment of elation when we scored the winning goal. I pictured that moment in my mind. I would do my best to make it real.

Of course, I wasn't the only one digging deep and finding something new. Seamus, who had been pretty worn out, got his second wind. He stretched out those long legs of his and ate up the pitch like a kangaroo.

He easily cut me off and took possession of the ball, then raced for our goal. I wasn't even as worried about him as their striker, though. Vince looked ready, at least, if they got within scoring distance.

Seamus glanced over at the striker running abreast of him. He lashed his leg out for a pass. I reacted, pouncing on the space between them.

Only, Seamus faked me out.

CHAPTER 23
A Pat on the Back

"A pat on the back is just two feet away from a kick in the pants."

— Bobby "the Brain" Heenan

He kept on dribbling instead of passing, and my distraction made me fall behind. Seamus and the striker slowed down and moved laterally, trying to avoid our fullbacks.

Seamus passed to the striker, who smashed a corner shot in really low. The ball did that thing where it seemed to spin in a different direction than it traveled. Vince jogged up to it and then calmly put his cleats down on top of the leather to trap the ball.

The striker and Seamus smothered me, trying to block Vince from giving me the ball. They were treating me like the biggest threat on my team. That should have made me happy, I guess, but things had been easier when they underestimated me.

I shoved those thoughts out of my head. Paul said that

soccer is never supposed to be easy because nothing worth doing ever is. If they weren't going to make it easy on me, I should take it as a compliment and try a little bit harder.

Then I figured something out. I could use their fear of me to our team's advantage. While the two best offensive players on their side were worried about me, they couldn't try and get into a scoring position themselves.

I broke hard for the right corner, and they followed me. I hoped they couldn't see me grin because they totally fell for my trap. Vince threw the ball in near Percival, who only dribbled a few feet before passing it toward the enemy goal.

Seamus and the striker realized they'd been had. They both zipped after the ball, leaving me in the dust. I let them get ahead, and then pushed myself as hard as I could.

The looks on their faces when I ran past them were so hilarious. They both tried to pick up the speed, too. But they had been hauling a lot of extra weight up and down the field all day. My smaller body worked to my advantage.

That didn't mean I wasn't tired as all get out. I concentrated on breathing evenly, instead of gasping like a landed fish. I felt the grass under my cleats, the wind going through my sweat-soaked hair, and fell into a kind of trance.

This was the zone. It had to be. I'd never really felt like I'd made the zone before, even on my best day. But everything just clicked. Everything made sense. I could see the Butterfield fullbacks harassing the ball away from Han, and I knew just what move they would make next.

I veered hard to the right and raced sideways along the field about ten yards from the center line. As I predicted, the fullbacks worked together to tackle the ball away from Han. Then they passed it between themselves for another twenty feet before Daniel and Alex caught up to them.

The left fullback smacked the ball toward Seamus, but he hadn't put himself in quite the right position. I easily intercepted the pass and dribbled sideways along the pitch the way I had just come.

I turned toward their goal line when I needed the boundary line. My cleats were less than an inch from the powder as I dribbled. While being that close hemmed me in, it also meant Butterfield could only try a tackle from one side.

When I got about thirty feet from the goal, I had five Butterfield players all gunning for me. I snapped my leg back like I was about to go for another goal.

They fell for my trap. Everyone moved as if there would be a throw-in from the keeper because, this time, he was paying attention. A shot from that far off isn't impossible, but it's not likely to score.

Only I didn't kick the ball toward the goal. I smacked it with the side of my foot instead, sending it over to a waiting Alex. My pass went a little high, but he let the ball smack his chest and then recovered it on the ground.

Alex dribbled about ten feet before the Butterfield corner came in and slid through the grass, smacking the ball out of Alex's reach. Alex jumped over the corner's leg, avoiding a trip but losing possession of the ball.

The Butterfield caught the pass and ran the ball toward our half of the pitch. With our team formation skewed toward offense, he had about fifty feet of wide open space between him and our goal.

Percival and our other fullback moved to intercept. Seamus and their winger joined the striker, forming a titanic triad that threatened to roll right over our defensive line.

Percival tried to tackle, but the striker batted the ball

over to the winger, who continued to charge our goal. The rest of us were catching up, but I already knew the winger would have plenty of time to take his shot.

I really hoped Vince was ready. The winger came in on the right side of the goal. I could tell by his posture he was going to fake to the left and then kick right. Our only chance was if Vince saw it, too.

The winger took his shot, pulling off a quick double-footed feint before smashing the ball into the right side of the goal. Vince flopped onto his knees and took the ball on his face and neck.

His arms snapped out and grabbed the ball, though, hugging it to his chest. The crowd went crazy at the wild save. I stopped running and hung out near the middle of the pitch. I had a feeling that I would be needed near the Butterfield goal soon.

Vince went for a throw-in, tossing the ball to Han. But Seamus snuck up and stole the pass, shooting the ball quickly to the striker.

The striker drove a shot in for the upper left corner of the goal, where Vince was weakest. Vince grunted as he jumped into the air, using his hands to deflect the shot.

The ball shot back onto the field and headed for the boundary line. A half dozen players from both teams attacked the ball, trying to get possession. I lost track of the ball for just a moment, and when I found it again, Han had taken possession.

He shot a long, hard kick down the pitch. Daniel was a little closer than I and took up dribbling. I did my best to block and run interference for him, but Daniel wasn't quite as fast as he had been at the beginning of the game.

The Butterfield winger snuck up and tackled him, stealing the ball away before I could close the gap. But Alex came in from the other side and tackled the ball away from the winger. He drove hard for the goal, long legs flying over the sun heated grass.

Alex smashed a goal shot from fifteen feet out, and man did that ball fly. I could barely follow it as it zipped in a blur toward the bottom right corner of Butterfield's goal.

Their keeper threw himself in front of the ball in the nick of time. It bounced off his back, did a lazy, slow roll, and wound up out of bounds.

The refs blew their whistles, and I thought it would be for a throw-in for our side. But to my surprise, it was a time-out.

"What's going on, Coach?" I asked Coach Johnson as I made it to the sidelines. "Who called the time-out?"

"The officials did. They want all you kids to get a hydration break."

I gritted my teeth in frustration. Sure, I was thirsty, but I could have managed. The time-out had completely broken our momentum. Worse, it had jolted me out of the zone. I didn't feel like I was in the zone, at least.

But when I got a look at some of my fellow players, I understood why the refs were concerned. It was hot enough to fry an egg on the sidewalk, and we'd been playing like there was no tomorrow. I decided the best thing to do would be to get as much rest as I could.

"Does anyone need to use the potty?" Coach Stan asked.

"The potty? He called it the potty," Daniel snickered.

"Alas, I have sweated out all the moisture in my body, and my bladder remains empty," Percival said.

We finished our sports drinks, and I have to admit, I

felt better. But so did everyone else, including the other team. When we re-took the field for Alex's throw-in, they all looked a lot less gassed than they had.

I checked the game clock. There was less than a minute left! I wanted to be mad at the referees for forcing the break with so little time left. I mean, it seemed like doing that favored our opponents.

If we were going to score a goal and win, we had to do it pretty much right now.

Alex threw-in to me. I immediately dribbled for the enemy goal, but four players moved to block my path. I glanced around, looking for someone free, and then passed backward to Han. He had been the only one I could hope to reach without an intercept.

Han dribbled diagonally, moving toward the enemy goal but also trying to avoid the mosh pit of players scrambling to catch up with him.

Han passed to Daniel, who smashed a shot at their goal. The keeper raced over and smacked the ball away with the edge of his hand, barely keeping us from making the score.

The ball bounced like cray cray, sailing like thirty feet into the air. Most of the players from both teams bunched up where it was expected to land. I stayed out of it, putting myself between the ball and our half of the pitch in case one of their team got possession.

The ball fell down like a meteor, leading to an insane scramble. If there hadn't been so much stuff going on at once, the refs would have definitely blown their whistles and carded people on both sides. I saw Han, normally a really chill guy, grab the Butterfield fullback and yank his jersey until they both fell.

But the other team was in on it, too. Seamus clotheslined

Daniel with his shoulder, sending our striker head over heels to crash in a painful heap on the grass. At least six other players went down, though mostly from trips and stumbles and not fouls.

Alex and the striker both went to recover the ball. The striker went for the tackle when Alex got there first, but Alex was ready to block. The ball kind of squirted up into the air between them and they both fell down.

The ball went up, seemed to hover for a second in the blue sky, and then tumbled back down. I could see it would land in the middle of the melee. Probably the refs would force a kickoff or a throw-in, if no one was in a position to recover it.

That's when I slipped back into the zone. I knew what I had to do. Normally, I would be terrified of doing such a risky move, especially in a championship game.

But I didn't hesitate. I ran up on the pile of squirming players lying on the grass. Bunching up my legs, I sprang up into the air, twisting my body around as I flew.

I had to time it just right. My momentum twisted me in a total circle before I lashed out with my foot. My flying round kick struck home, sending the ball like a rocket ship toward the enemy net.

Their keeper's eyes got wide as the sun. He panicked, throwing himself at the ball just a little bit too soon. The ball sailed an inch past his gloved fingers and sank into the net.

That was the last thing I saw before I landed in the grass. Hard. My cheek bounced off the turf, and my vision got dark around the edges for a second. I could hear a lot of people shouting and moving around me, but it took me a little bit to remember where I was.

"Get up," someone practically screamed, grabbing my

arm. For an instant, I thought maybe Seamus was coming to finish me off since I'd scored another goal. Instead, I looked up into the face of Daniel. His lip was swollen and bleeding, but he smiled anyway.

"What happened?" I asked, still feeling kind of loopy after bouncing my head off the pitch.

"You just won, you idiot! There's eight seconds left on the clock. The refs are calling it!"

"We won?" I asked, barely able to believe it.

The whole team swarmed me, shouting my name.

They lifted me onto their shoulders and carried me off the pitch. I looked around, more scared and confused than happy. What the heck was going on?

"Max Goalman is the MVP," Coach Stan said. "Way to go, Kid."

"Good job, Goalman," Coach Johnson said. His smile faded. "But don't get cocky! You're still green as grass and have a ton to learn."

"I know, Coach," I said as the team hoisted me around again.

The refs called for an end to our little parade. They lined us up for the post-game handshake. I was a little intimidated when it was my turn to shake Seamus' hand, but he just grunted.

"You won this time, but we'll get you next year," he said as he let go of my hand. I checked to make sure none of my fingers were broken, just in case.

"Maybe you will if you play harder instead of trying to cheat all the time," I said back.

"You're supposed to say good game," one of the refs snapped. "Move along."

I guessed that I would be seeing Seamus again in other games and other tournaments. I would be ready for him next time, though.

The locker room echoed with happy cheering. After the arena, I thought nothing would hurt my ears. Boy was I wrong.

I joined in on the hollering. If you can't beat 'em, join 'em. My dad says that a lot.

"Settle down," Coach Johnson said, but he didn't sound angry about it. He waited another few minutes, I think to give us time to get all the screaming out of our systems. Then he blew sharply on his whistle.

"All right, all right, we're all excited. And I am incredibly proud of each and every one of you," Coach Johnson said. "But we're not done yet. As the winning team, we'll be expected to attend the official trophy ceremony. They'll also be picking the tournament MVP."

I perked up at that. I played pretty good, but had I been good enough to earn that honor?

"Don't get your hopes up, Maxwell," Percival whispered in my ear. "In the thirty years this tournament has gone on, they've almost never given MVP to a player from the winning team."

"They haven't? That doesn't make any sense."

"I think they want to spread the accolades around."

I didn't know what the word accolades meant until later when I looked it up. I tried to spell it with an O first. But I got the general gist. We had won the tournament and the trophy, so the judges would give the MVP to another team to give them something to be happy about.

While I understood, it also made me feel like they were treating us like little kids. I wouldn't want to be called MVP because someone thought I could feel bad if I didn't. I wanted to actually earn the title.

"So you all have about twenty minutes to get washed up. Coach Bobby is on the way with clean uniforms for everyone."

"Why do we have to change?" Daniel asked. "On TV, the pros stand there with mud and blood on their uniforms."

"Well, this ain't the pros, and we ain't on TV, are we?" Coach Johnson snorted. "You're a good player, Daniel. You'd be a great one if you got that attitude of yours under control."

Daniel looked like he just sucked on a lemon. I figured that Coach didn't know Daniel had actually turned over a new leaf. He was almost nice here lately.

"So get cleaned up, and try to conduct yourselves with some dignity when we get back on the field for the ceremony."

We washed up and put on the clean uniforms. Only one problem, though. Coach Bobby brought fresh clothes but not socks, so we wound up putting our sweaty, stinky socks on clean feet.

I didn't care. My mind still glowed with our victory. That game was the hardest one I'd ever played. My parents told me that you really appreciate the wins that come with effort more. I supposed that was true. I felt proud of my team. We'd come into the tournament as one of the bottom seeds and wound up winning the whole thing.

After a while, we all settled down. All of us talked excitedly about the game. There was a lot of the old "Did you see when I..." and "I can't believe that you..." going around. But we weren't jumping or hollering anymore.

When Coach Johnson came to get us for the ceremony, I got real nervous all of a sudden. My family would be watching. What if someone expected me to talk? I hated public speaking, something I shared with my dad.

The crowd applauded when we took the field and lined up near the center. Somebody set up a podium, as well as a table and chairs while we were in the locker room. La Forge's headmaster was going to give a speech. I really hoped it would be shorter than the first one.

Spoiler alert: It was not.

Like most grown-ups, he couldn't just talk about the game or the tournament. No, he had to try and link everything back to working hard in class and being good people. Blah, blah, blah. My belly rumbled and growled. All I wanted was to eat.

But when they brought the trophies out, I got excited all over again. The headmaster still droned on like a bee hive, but at least I had something to look at.

The headmaster finally finished his speech, and people applauded. Hard. I think they were just as glad the windbag was done as I was.

If I thought my wait was almost over, I sure was wrong. I forgot they had to present the girl's trophies, too. I was going to clap and be polite, but then I saw my nemesis on the winning team.

"Augusta Lorena Sanchez Villa-Lobos Ramírez?" I sputtered. "You guys won?"

"Yeah, duh. We won because we're the best." She sneered at me, stopping on her way to the platform to accept the trophy with the girl's team. "And I don't mean we're just the best girls' team. We're the best team from Caldwell Academy, period."

I shook my head as she walked up to join her team.

236

"Man, that girl drives me crazy," I growled.

Percival laughed. I glared at him.

"What's so funny?"

"Ah, Maxwell. Me think the lady doth protest too much."

I groaned.

"Will you speak English?"

He sighed.

"I'm trying to say, without sounding like a crude peasant, that all that anger you have for her is hiding something else."

I finally figured it out. I had to laugh, so hard my sides hurt.

"You've got to be kidding! I hate her guts! She's the one who made everyone call me Mr. Snoogie."

He smirked, and that made me even angrier. The girls' team got their trophy. I clapped to be polite, because my parents were watching.

Then it was our turn. I got so nervous I almost threw up on the way to the stage. We stood behind the headmaster as he handed the trophy to Coach Johnson.

Coach Johnson thanked the headmaster, held the trophy over his head, and smiled huge. Then he set it down and motioned for us to come over.

The whole team rushed up to feel the trophy. It was huge! Almost as tall as Coach Johnson. Shiny gold columns and a statuette of a man playing soccer dazzled my eyes. I mean, sure, it probably wasn't real gold or anything, but it looked cool.

"She's going to look great in our trophy case at Caldwell

Academy," Coach Johnson said.

"Are we done, Coach?" I asked. "I'm starving, and I think my parents are looking for me."

"Your parents are fine, Goalman," he snapped. "We're NOT done here. There's still the MVP presentation."

To my surprise, the headmaster gave up the podium to another speaker. It took me a second to recognize him because he had a lot more gray hair and a beard, but then I figured it out.

"Is that Jean-Luc Gaspard?" I whispered to Daniel.

"Who the heck is that?" Daniel asked.

I sighed and whispered the same question to Percival.

"Indeed it is, Maxwell. He was listed as the honorary presenter of the MVP award. Didn't you read that on the tournament's official website?"

"No, I was spending all my time training for the tournament. I didn't have time to read the website."

"Well, if you had, then — "

"Can it, or you're washing all the toilets in the Cannon Stadium when we get back," Coach Johnson said in a harsh whisper.

We got real quiet. Gaspard had been to the World Cup finals at least seven times. One of those, he was the championship game MVP. I'd always thought he was a good historical player to study because he never limited himself to one position. He played everything, even tending the goal.

"How is everyone doing?" he asked in a thick French accent. "Good! I am super excited to have the honor of presenting the tournament MVP award."

He gestured at the plaque. While the trophy was for the whole team, coaches included, that plaque could be exclusively for the player named MVP. I wondered who it would be? Probably someone on Butterfield's team.

"Now, there have been many great players over the last few days," Gaspard said. "But there's one player who stood out. One player who overcame injury and his own self-doubt to become a champion. I don't say this very often, but this kid, he's going places. Like World Cup kind of places."

The crowd applauded. My stomach growled. I just wanted to hang with my parents and eat!

"Stand up straight, Goalman," Coach Johnson said. "If your parents don't scare you enough, you should know there are international talent scouts who've been watching the entire tourney. You don't want to look like a slacker, do you?"

"No, Coach," I said, shaking my head. I stood up straighter. Fortunately, it sounded like Gaspard was finally winding up his speech.

"What more can you say about the guy?" he said, which made the crowd laugh. "Without further ado, here he is, your tournament MVP, Maxwell Goalman."

Man, I didn't even hear him call my name. I only realized he meant me when Percival stomped on my toes with his cleats.

"Maxwell, go and collect your award."

I blinked and looked at him in shock. When I checked out the arena, everyone was looking at me and clapping. Me? The MVP? I hadn't thought it would happen.

My legs shook bad when I walked back up onto that stage.

Before, I'd been with the whole team. Now, I was all alone with a legend I admired.

"Here you go, Maxwell," Gaspard said.

"I'm not sure I deserve this."

He scoffed.

"You deserve it. Nobody worked harder or played better than you. It was your effort, and not just God-given talent, that won you the MVP award."

Gaspard handed me the plaque. It felt heavier than it looked. I tucked it under my arm so I could shake his huge, hairy hand.

"But remember," Gaspard said. "Always remain humble and grateful! Look at how well it's worked out for moi."

I laughed.

"I will, I promise. Thank you, sir."

I shook the headmaster's hand, too, and a couple of other people I didn't know who must have been tournament bigwigs.

I stopped before I left the stage and held the award over my head. I smiled so hard my cheeks hurt. The crowd cheered loud when I lifted up my MVP award for some reason. Maybe they were happy the headmaster was finally done talking.

Or was he? He stepped up to the mike, and we all groaned, but all he did was thank all the participants and audience and tell us good night.

"Well, you got the MVP, Mr. Snoogie," Daniel said. "And I'm not saying you didn't earn it. But what happens now?"

"Now? Now I'm going to demolish a pizza!"

CHAPTER 24
The Triumph of Mr. Snoogie

"They don't think it be like it is, but it do. Do be do be do."

— Oscar Gamble

My mom hugged me so tight she almost broke my ribs.

"My baby!" she said, almost in tears. "I'm so proud of you! You were amazing."

I tried to gasp for air. Over my mom's shoulder, I saw Emma filming us with her cell phone. Oh, good grief, I hope that video doesn't wind up on the internet. It was bad enough everyone called me Mr. Snoogie; being a mama's boy would be that much worse.

"Good job, Max," Dad said. "And sorry about the belch."

I glared at him.

"You should be," I said, but it came out like a squeak because of Mom's bearhug.

Mom finally let me go.

"Gee, Mom, can we go eat? I'm starving."

"Of course, we can go out to eat. Where do you want to go?"

"Anywhere there's pizza."

Dad chuckled and dug out his cell phone, looking up the local pizza places around La Forge Academy. He found one that said it had free dessert pizza, which made me super happy.

When the smell of the pizzeria hit my nostrils, I started drooling. Fortunately, they gave us some breadsticks while we waited for our pies. I gobbled up an entire basket all by myself.

I probably ate half the first pizza by myself and washed it down with a ton of soda pop. My mom and dad had a bunch of questions, but not about the tournament. They wanted to know if I was making friends, doing good with school, all of that stuff that parents worry about.

"I've made a lot of friends," I said. "I mean, there's Percival, and Alex, and, um, Daniel."

"Do you have any friends who aren't on the soccer team?" Angela asked sweetly.

"Um, sure, I do," I said.

"Of course, he has friends outside of his soccer club, honey," Mom said. "He's friends with that nice Lobo girl."

I choked on my pizza, and had to cough up into a napkin. I looked at my mother in horror.

"Nice? Nice? Lobo isn't nice. She's like a demon! And

she is definitely not my friend, no matter what she told you."

Dad laughed.

"He's at that age," he said to my mom with a wink. "Girls, yuck."

"You're darn tootin', Girls, Yuck," I said.

The dessert pizza arrived right about then, and we stopped talking and started eating. There was whipped cream crust, and chocolate chip cookie dough made up the majority of it. Normally, I would have worried about all that sugar.

But after burning like a billion calories during the tournament, I figured it couldn't hurt.

Mom and Dad had another surprise for me. Instead of riding back to Caldwell on the bus, they were taking me home for a few days.

"Mom, you can't do that! My teachers are super hardcore. They won't let me make up the work."

"Yes, they will. I already called them."

I couldn't argue with that. It was nice to go home, I have to admit. But even so, I kept thinking about how much I couldn't wait to get back onto the Cannon soccer pitch.

I spent a few days catching up on this journal and hanging with my parents. The last day before I was supposed to return to the academy, I got something in the mail. The snail mail, not email.

Mom handed me a shiny black and white envelope. It felt heavy, like it was made of really thick, quality paper. I was almost afraid to tear into it, the lion logo on the front was so pretty.

But I had to see what was inside. Mom and Dad stood behind me, reading over my shoulder. They hate it when I do that to them, but that's how parents are.

"What does it say, Max?" Dad said, squinting. I guess he'd forgotten his glasses again.

"It's from the Lancaster Lions," I said in awe.

"The who?" Mom asked.

"The Lions are one of the most famous international youth clubs anyone has ever heard of. And they want me to try out..."

My heart sank when I read the rest of the letter.

"When I'm old enough," I finished with a sigh.

"It's only a year or two, Max," Mom said. "This is huge."

"Yeah, you're right," I thought, remembering what Gaspard told me. Always be humble and grateful. "I'm super grateful that they're interested in me after just one tournament."

"That's the spirit," Dad said, mussing my hair.

Emma snickered at me.

"Go get 'em, Mr. Snoogie."

I decided I would forgive her. Just this once.

Made in the USA
Las Vegas, NV
13 October 2024